OMG...!

You're Still Single, So Where the Hell Is Your Lemonade?

OMG...!

You're Still Single, So Where the Hell Is Your Lemonade?

A Memoir by
Sheryl L. Bradford

SLB Publishing

Bradford, Sheryl L.
Omg...You're Still Single, So Where the Hell Is Your Lemonade? /Sheryl L. Bradford.

ISBN 978-0692133439

Single women—Psychology. Interpersonal relations. Single women—Religious life.
Unless otherwise indicated, all Scripture quotations are from the New Living Translation. All rights reserved.
Scripture Quotations marked *KJV* are from the Holy Bible, King James Version, 1979. All rights reserved.

Printed in the United States of America
First Edition
Book cover designed by Jennifer Olsson

For my mother, Delores T. Bradford Adams, who never ever asked, "So, Sheryl, you're still not married?" She loved her children for who they are, and she kept me laughing through some of the toughest days of my single life. Miss you, Momma!

CONTENTS

Foreword...13

Introduction 17

Part I: The Bitter Truth 27

    Chapter 1: Dispelling the Myth...............29

    Chapter 2: "So You're Still Not Married?" 45

    Chapter 3: The "Terrible Thirties"...........55

    Chapter 4: Cinderella Turns Forty 67

    Chapter 5: Waiting to Exhale!..................81

Part II: From Bitter to Sweet.............................99

    Chapter 6: Radical Gratitude....................101

    Chapter 7: The Misplaced Lives of Eve 109

    Chapter 8: A Table for One, Please! 119

    Chapter 9: Orgasm, A Girl's Best Friend............131

    Chapter 10: Beauty Does Matter! 141

    Chapter 11: The Acid Analysis 149

Epilogue 157

Acknowledgements 165

The Lemon Gloss...167

Filmography..171

About the Author 173

Notes 175

My journal read, "The day had arrived that I always dreaded—forty—still single. I had fought a good fight, now I had to face the music…and the tune would not be, 'Here Comes the Bride.'"

May 26, 1999

FOREWORD

My mother, Delores T. Bradford Adams, passed away in January of 2011. She was an inspiration to our family and the community in which we lived. She had uncanny strength and wisdom. It is only fitting that she writes this foreword for my first attempt as an author. She did, after all, give me my favorite book (still to this day) Green Eggs and Ham *by Dr. Seuss.*

Shelzy, as I affectionately called Sheryl, was my second daughter. Early on she loved to read, just as I did. You know that reading and writing go hand in hand. In fact, as she got older we worried that she was closing herself off from the real world a bit too much to enjoy this activity. But it worked to her good since she always did very well in school and it helped develop her into a well-rounded individual. She could talk about anything and she loved talking, much to her teachers' dismay.

Though I have passed on, I am not surprised that she has written this book. She has made me proud many times over. I admired her intelligence, attractiveness, and ability to wear anything and look like a million dollars. (Why not, she got those things from me.) She was one of a very few African-Americans to become fashion buyers for the prominent southeastern retailer Belk Stores Inc. (during the 80s), she obtained three degrees with honors, and later at forty-something, she bravely left a secure job and relocated to pursue a faith-inspired calling for her life.

Sheryl is right…I never asked her once why she never married. However, I was always concerned that those romance novels she read had distorted her view of relationships. I believe that she would always have unrealistic expectations. But I just wanted her to be happy and hoped that she would not be alone. I knew that she had a strong sense of herself since I taught her early on to never ever wish to be someone else. I joked that if you could be "a fly on the wall" in other people's lives you would be surprised at what they go through! And I knew she lived by my saying that "it is not what happens to you that matters, but how you respond to what happens to you." Guess she is passing that message on!

Pretty clever, this lemonade thing. She always had a great imagination and she has always genuinely cared about folk. Maybe too much. When she was younger, I watched her and thought, "Sheryl is gonna get hurt and disappointed a lot." She had great expectations for herself and other people.

If her high standards for most things hold true, y'all should enjoy this book. Of course, my Shelzy does know a little something about being single. Tough times for her—

she didn't always use good judgment—those romance books, you see. But she always sprung back! A lot to do with her faith.

I used to tell her this story about a black female abolitionist that lived during the early years of slavery. Whenever she experienced the trials of life, the abolitionist would say, "Can't worry about that now, gotta keep on going, keep on pushing!" When you have life goals with great purpose you got to rise above obstacles to accomplish them. Hope my Shelzy remembers this as she keeps on making me proud!

Delores T. Bradford Adams

INTRODUCTION

Hey, y'all, listen up! First, I want to thank you for making the decision to join this conversation. What...you don't think we can converse through the written word? You just wait! It's nothing better than a bunch of women getting together for a **kickback**. You gonna love it! So what should I call you—ladies—sisters? Some of you are young enough to be my daughters (Yes, I'm comfortable enough to admit that). You know, why don't I just call you "girls" like Helen Gurley Brown did in the 1962 cult classic *Sex and the Single Girl*, which was re-issued in 2003 because of its timeless message.[*] Yes...**"girls"**...it's perfect cuz before this chick fest is over you'll realize that we all remain girls throughout our lives! Shoot, call me what you want, "ma'am, Miss" I still feel like a girl even at 50-something! Hear me now, girls, I have put off having this conversation with you—single women—since I was forty. Really, I have put the idea on the backburner many times. You see, I thought, "nobody cares about a middle-aged woman that has never married." But the urge to share my story remained with me. The urge intensified a couple of years after celebrating my fortieth birthday when I began taking devotional walks early in the morning and later recording my reflections in my journal. Getting older and remaining single was no cake walk for me. I know many of you know what I'm talking about. I had dreamed since adolescence of finding someone special and sharing my life with him. So I spent many years of my early adult life tormented by my quest to make this dream a reality. Yes, I literally use the word *torment* as I recall my attempts to make sure I did not become a forgotten old single woman! I was terrified of what this failure would imply about me as a female. It was tough enough for women in their thirties (during the 80s) to wed; here I was at age forty, still single. For me, this was a nightmare!

Looking back, I wonder if I cursed myself. During my last year of undergraduate study I jumped the gun—I purchased a complete set of china, crystal glasses, stainless flatware, and cookware from a vendor visiting our campus. Was it foreshadowing? Did I somehow know that years would pass and I would remain single? Did I subconsciously sense that it would be the only way I would own these items—traditional gifts for the bride? They remain packaged and stored minus the cookware that I have used preparing meals for a number of discarded Mr. Rights. Was I too anxious—was I unrealistic to prepare for "domestic bliss" before I had someone to marry?

Maybe. But things haven't changed that much—like me—most women—most of you in fact—desire and plan to marry. The average age for women has increased to 26.1 but marriage is still a common phenomenon.[*] In fact, weddings are a billion-dollar industry in America![*] After graduation (1981), and during the late 80s and 90s everyone around me was getting married. Y'all know the story. By the time I was thirty, most of my childhood, high school, and college friends were married. To my disdain, I was the only child in my family that didn't get married, and the only granddaughter amongst fifteen not to as well. You know what they say, "If I had a dollar for every wedding or shower gift I purchased…?" So I definitely was not the only one who fantasized about marriage. Though there are some who would say that the hundreds (perhaps thousands) of Harlequin romance novels that I read during adolescence didn't help, nor did watching romantic movies on television starring Doris Day, Rock Hudson, and Cary Grant into the wee morning hours. (Some of you don't know who I'm talking about…just insert Cameron Diaz or Kate Hudson and their list of leading men.) Both activities probably contributed to my distorted idea of love and marriage. But a lot of folk have a distorted idea of love and marriage—just take a look at the current divorce and remarriage rates in our country.[*]

Thankfully, single women today are not as stigmatized for never marrying as we were in times past, but there are still clear signs that we equate our self-worth with marriage and having children. In the twenty-first century, you would think that women attending major colleges and universities would have developing their careers and making strides in the world as their primary focus by age thirty. Not according to a survey conducted by Her Campus Media, parent company of Hercampus.com (an online community for college women) which revealed that 85.1% of the 2600 respondents from 677 different colleges and universities want to be married by age thirty.[*] The survey appeared in the August 2012 online version of *Self* magazine. In the article, CEO Stephanie Kaplan states that, "Today's college women want it all—the prestigious degrees, the dream job, and the dream life, which for the vast majority of them include marriage and kids." 46.5% of the young women from the classes of 2012-2015 desired to be married between the ages 25-27, 20.9% of them chose the age group 28-30, and 17.1% wanted to wed by the time they turn 25.

And what about this obsession y'all have with the lives of pop culture personalities and their marriages? The tabloids can't get enough of heir to the English throne William and his wife Kate, (and now brother Henry and his nuptials in May) or Hip-hop royalty Jay-Z and Beyoncé. Even the hoax of a marriage between Kanye West and Kim Kardashian (that's my opinion) is a mainstay on the covers of reputable entertainment magazines. Adding to the mayhem is the obsession (I am not guilty, of course) with television reality shows depicting countless exhibitions of dysfunctional wives, brides, and marriages. The *Atlanta Housewives* ain't one of the top shows for nothing. Even stronger evidence of your fixation is the success of the number one rated relationship reality show, *The Bachelor*.[*] Makes sense, it's an extreme example of what women will endure to find someone to marry. Regrettably most of it is shameful—the display of several women vying for the attention of one eligible man—their willingness to participate just a testament to how desperate we are to become Mrs. Somebody. We should remember that a man created and produced the show. What man wouldn't want twenty-plus women to agree to be played with and dumped? Yeah, right…I'm sure he had pure intentions. The show has yet to produce a true love match!

Recently, two male authors have even decided to cash in on the plight of the single woman. Both books, *He's Not That Into You* by Greg Behrendt and Liz Tuccillo (2004) and *Act Like a Lady, Think Like a Man*, by Steve Harvey with Denene Millner (2009) have been made into major movies. Undoubtedly, both authors owe their success to the frantic need women have for discovering what it takes to get their man—any man—to the altar. (Check out my review of both books in Chapter Eleven). Another subtle act of desperation is the willingness of our African-American sisters aged 25-44 to engage in risky sexual behavior. More than half of the growing number of Aids cases in the U.S. is amongst this group.[*] Some may disagree, but it is my fear that most of these women, especially those 25-35, have risked their lives (yielding to risky sexual activity) in pursuit of finding a mate. It's been thoroughly documented that this demographic will remain single longer than any other and may never marry (55%, almost 6 out of 10).[*] These statistics surely increase the anxiety and desperation for those desiring to wed.

So why should y'all listen to me? For one thing, even at fifty-something, I still got it going on! I'm PHAT—Pretty Hot and Tempting. I know—that's an old, old acronym,

LOL! Seriously though, I struggled through my late twenties and thirties trying to grasp what was wrong with me. Others wondered as well. They wanted to know how someone who is smart, sexy, funny, sophisticated, well-rounded (and not conceited) remained single. Truthfully, I tried unsuccessfully to have the life that those around me had obtained and I minimized my own journey. Finally, exhausted, I reached my forties and began to accept my fate. Not that I will never marry, (that's always possible) but that my life's timetable would gravely differ from those around me. Getting to this revelation has not been easy, to say the least. Still, I bet you think that along my journey I learned what a girl's gotta do to get hitched. Yeah—some of y'all would probably pay me big bucks for that **411**! Sorry, girls, even at fifty-something I have no knowledge of any absolute truth or wisdoms for our dilemma, if there is any. What I get to do with my book is to explore my journey being single and hope that something I share will make your journey easier. I have been single all of my adult life and I have no children. But I have loved and been loved; I have hurt and been hurt; I have used and been used; I have disappointed and been disappointed; I have misled and been misled; I have forgiven and been forgiven— as well, I have dreamed and hoped, cried, and despaired; I have experienced passion and pain, desperation and disdain.

And still, "I rise."* The truth is when I look in the mirror, I still see that same girl…waiting, hoping, desiring. I still am collecting items for my trousseau; I know y'all probably need to look that word up. And I have not burned my wedding plans—even though the bag that holds it together has been taped over and over again! Of course, along the way I have learned that there are other dimensions to my life—other passions. But I don't have to apologize for my desire—still—to have "*An Affair to Remember.*" (Y'all know Debra Kerr and Cary Grant.) Oh, I forgot, think of the romance between Barbra Streisand and James Brolin. With every breath I take, I know that there is still time for my happily ever after. My overall message to women struggling with being single is just that. But first, we must celebrate who we are—our entire journey—because it makes us who we are. My experiences living single through my twenties, thirties, forties are a part of my mystique. I delight now in sharing a bit of the wisdom I acquired from the "joy and pain" of being single. Since we were little girls, most of us have imagined ourselves falling in love and getting married. But what do we do when our dreams are deferred or never materialize? My hope is that my sharing will help single women to **re-imagine** their lives, create new realities for themselves—simply put, **make lemonade**!

So what do I mean—make lemonade? It is similar to a lesson I learned from my mother when I was a young girl. This lesson transformed my perspective of life so much that it became more than a saying. It became a way of life—my way of rising above any challenge life offered. Y'all have probably heard the saying, "It is not what happens to you in life that matters, but how you respond to what happens to you." Credit is given to Dale Carnegie, American writer and advocate of self-improvement, as the first person to coin the phrase "When fate hands us a lemon…make lemonade."[*] I believe this statement from Carnegie expresses the essence of the lesson I learned. So when life gives you lemons, (years living alone, dead-end relationships) you can choose to have a sour attitude about them or—re-imagine your situation, you can make lemonade!

In the first half of the book I examine what I call the "stuff"—**lemons**—the single woman will face as she strives to achieve a well-balanced life unmarried. She will be challenged by external, as well as internal, forces that at times will be overwhelming. To varying degrees, single women will suffer, emotionally, socially, and spiritually as they interact with their families, peers, those of their faith, co-workers, and greater society as a whole.

The second half of the book is a recipe for turning lemons into lemonade. The single woman must intentionally tackle the grief that comes with her lifestyle. She deserves a fulfilling and rewarding life, but she must create it! If she remains single for many years, at each life passage, she must re-imagine what she desires for herself—I believe that's my "genius."

To end the book, I had a little fun. I responded to the "how to getta man" advice from three bestselling authors. If you were like me, you have read countless books on the subject. It's my payback for no **ROI**!

Girls, I may have stated it too mildly earlier, but let me make it clear, "I have longed to have this conversation with you." So much so, that I believe that it was my destiny to write this book and it's my hope that through you (my reading audience) many others will be empowered. You will find while reading that I take a few liberties with the English language, creating my own terminology to initiate us into sharing this examination of our lives. As well, throughout the chapters, I use text/twitter shorthand, hoping to keep the attention of y'all younger singles and of course to show off the fact that "I know what's up!" I hope the use of the two strategies does not seem awkward or pretentious. For y'all less tech savvy readers, at the back of the book I provide definitions for the single life jargon and the shorthand (both will appear in bold type when first used) in what I call the **Lemon Gloss**, (glossary) for ease of reading. I don't want any single woman left out of our conversation!

Let me be honest, girls, writing this book has not been an easy task. Taking the trip down memory lane can be painful. Revisiting the entries in my journal during one of the toughest times of my life was hard. It is difficult being transparent—revealing one's vulnerabilities, disappointments, and failures, even when you know it will do others good. But I have been in the midst of younger and older single women and I have heard their stories. I have sensed their desire and longing so reminiscent of my own. So know one thing for sure, I bring no remorse or sadness to this endeavor. It has been therapeutic, and it is my desire that the book will not only advise, but also entertain and inspire.

Finally, as you read along you will notice bold crosses (✛) throughout the book's passages. Because my experiences and perspective of life have been informed by my journey as a Christian I decided to accommodate my Christian sisters with what I call Christian sidebars. Undeniably, my ability to reshape the circumstances of my life is directly related to my spiritual development over many years. These sidebars highlight tenants of our faith and will be listed at the end of each chapter. But to be clear to all readers—from all backgrounds and persuasions—the main focus of this book has not been to evangelize—but to empower! Its message can apply to anyone seeking answers in the human quest for wholeness. So the book is actually two in one—a secular memoir/ guide interlaced with a spiritual one. **G2G,** girls, let's get to squeezing those lemons, Chapter One— Dispelling the Myth!

Part I
The Bitter Truth

Chapter One

Dispelling the Myth

Girl...who is she? What's her name? You know the one; that married relative, friend, acquaintance, neighbor, or co-worker who makes your single life seem so tragic. Her life appears to be so perfect. Did she steal the man you were supposed to marry? Have the children you should have had? Live in the home you should have built? Drive the car you ought to be driving, or take the vacations you should have taken? Yeah...I know...she makes you sick! But stop pressing your nose against the window of her life long enough for some proper perspective. Girl, you're too close to the situation, LOL. If you step back far enough, you can view the whole picture and it ain't all of that—as they say! **(+1)**

Now after reading this first chapter, the critics will probably say that I appear to be a "hater" of married women and men. Trust me; I have celebrated at too many showers, weddings, and anniversaries of my cohorts to hate them.

Come over sometime and view the bulging photo albums and scrapbooks that contain the remnants of nuptials past. And men—let's just say I may need to pay off some friends to keep my escapades to themselves. Amazingly, even after all our strides in the workplace, politics, education, and the world at large we still buy into the propaganda. It starts with the fairy tale Cinderella (and others like it) and the race to the altar begins. The idea of marriage is so romanticized and entrenched in our culture that it is my intention in this chapter to deflate some of its appeal. Girls, I've got to come outta the gate with some stuff that would get you and I (remember I'm in this with you, I keep a copy of the movie *Ever After, A Cinderella Story* on my nightstand, **QL**) to compare single life with marriage realistically. Something tells me that everyone is not gonna like the way I have approached it.

Can we talk? Can we start by having an honest discussion about this lifestyle we covet, marriage? It's quite possible that it is not all that it appears to be. So how many of you enjoy wonderful nights of uninterrupted slumber? You know the kind, those that have you reaching for the snooze button over and over again the next morning. There is nothing like a good peaceful night of rest! **(+II)** Are you aware of the number of women who lose sleep every night because of their snoring husbands or significant others? I never realized that snoring could have such an adverse effect on relationships. That is until I started to hear experiences from married women who had to endure the distress of sleeping with a snoring mate. Statistics show that both men and women snore. But snoring is more a male problem, since forty per cent of them snore (Girls, that's 4 out of 10).* Plus, women are twice as likely to say that their partner's snoring is a problem. Sources claim that most couples prefer sleeping together despite this predicament. Personal accounts from friends and family suggest otherwise! Many couples sleep in separate rooms, and some marriages actually dissolve because of snoring.

Girls, just think, every night a number of women worry if and when they will get to sleep. Every night! And when they decide to travel, there's no going into another room. Trust me, not even ear plugs will work if you've got a serious snorer. Listen, I have a personal story to tell. I just hope the fellow doesn't read my book cuz he'll know I'm talking about him. Girls, the whole bed shook when he snored, and not even going into another room helped. As the night went on I became angry that he was keeping me from my rest. I honestly wanted to strangle him to make him stop. I cannot imagine bearing this interruption of sleep night after night. I'm not saying that I wouldn't marry a man who snores, if I loved him. But it's gonna take a lot more than love and so he might better have money too…shameful, right? Guess I sound selfish—but getting proper rest is vital to good health. I'm already thinking twice about this thing. Those of you gunning for marriage, better get your rest now! Chances are good that you won't get much of it once you snag Mr. Right.

Okayyyyy…it ain't that funny! I'll move on. During one episode of *Living Single*, a TV sitcom featuring a cast of four evolved single women, the question is asked, "What would life be without men?* Queen Latifah in her role as Khadijah James answers, "Women would be fat, happy, and there would be no crime." This statement suggests that women are driven to focus on their appearance and bodies because of the men in their lives. Queen may not be speaking for all women—but a heck of a lot of us. And if you are living with a man permanently, marriage I think they call it—then the drill of keeping yourself together never ends.

I have a bit of proof—I had one married co-worker to tell me that she can't wait 'til she has a day off home alone, so that she can eat whatever she wants. Can you imagine having to monitor what and how much you eat every day? Of course, this can be a good healthy thing, but girl you grown, he ain't your daddy! I couldn't believe it, but have you heard stories about married women who actually sleep with their make-up on or those who hide the fact that they have a full set of false teeth? Oh, the stress of hiding all our flaws. It reminds me of a scene from the movie, *I'm Gonna Git You Sucka* which depicts a hooker unveiling each disguised flaw one by one until she's hardly recognizable.*

No, I'm not calling married women whores! Back to my point. Now, if you're single, you get to lapse in the luxury of many days like the one I am about to describe. You see, some of the best days of my life are those spent doing absolutely nothing to enhance my appearance or to groom my body. Shhh...that's right; don't tell anyone but I get up, no shower, no tedious body care routine, no hassling with the hair, no fussing with the wardrobe, and definitely no makeup. Guess y'all think I'm nasty. (I do brush my teeth, Dr. Swain.) Of course, you just need to be careful which side of town you choose to run your errands. Every now and then I get stuck hiding in a grocery store from an old flame. You didn't think I would leave the house in this condition, did you? That's half the fun mocking the usual days of stress filled with these grooming activities.

What, you don't think this is such a big deal? I don't know too many married women, (those trying to keep their husbands interested), that would even walk around the house, not to mention leave their homes, as loosely groomed as I just described. And even if they were home alone all day, most of my married friends quickly groom themselves before their mates arrive. I can't count the number of times I saw my own mother remove her hair rollers right before my step-father arrived from work. Of course, there is a small downside to this good fortune. Some of you may ask, what if I meet Mr. Right? What if I am enjoying one of my loosely groomed days and miss out? Men after all are very visual creatures. Well, if he likes me at my worst, baby, he'll fall in love with me at my best! Girls, I'm kidding. Honestly, though, there's nothing like those carefree, groom-free days of being single. (I'm enjoying one, right now, while writing this!) Another downside; one of my close friends—who evidently had a high opinion of me—still to this day has not recovered from seeing me at the grocery during one of my groom-free days. She couldn't believe it. Some things we just can't live down! Whatever—the freedom from all the hassle is worth it.

Thus far, it sounds like I've had a blast being single? Doesn't it? **SMH**. It's just the first chapter, and I told you, I am a genius at this re-imagining thing. So let's get back to the wonderful life led by "Mrs. Smith." She probably got married by age 26.1 since that is the current average age for women in the U.S.; however, even after spending $20,000* plus on the wedding of her dreams, she, along with the other fifty-per-cent who got married will be divorced by 30.* Women are twice as likely to file for a divorce as men. Ironically, their dissatisfaction is often in the very areas which give cause for marriage. They feel alone and abandoned; their mate shows no interest in them, their mate is no longer romantic and just wants to have sex, or their mate lives like he is not married.* So, girls, maybe you won't be in the 50% that goes down this road. Keep reading; look at what's possible even if you stay married.

Girls, can we talk about infidelity, adultery? **(+III)** By the way, to be fair, only 17% of marriages end because of a cheating spouse. But guess what, 80% of married folk will cheat at least once during the marriage. More astounding is that 69% of married men cheat regularly, and 60% of women.* There are actually websites dedicated to helping married folk cheat. Ever heard of lonelycheatingwives.com? Girls, I couldn't believe it. What happened to "happily ever after?" Most of the research on the topic states that people are happier and healthier married. Can this be true when so many are seeking satisfaction outside their marriages? I know first-hand about the provocations and ill effects of adultery. But to protect the guilty and the innocent, I'll have to keep their stories to myself. Emotionally, women have a harder time with failed relationships. It is easy to conclude that many stay with cheating spouses to avoid even more mental stress. There are few stats that dispute the fact that men enjoy better mental and overall health being married. See, they win again, even in marriage, "It's a man's world!" But check this out my single sisters—the quality of our mental health compares to that of most married women and it surpasses it when examining women in bad marriages. I know...if you are thirty or younger, this news ain't turning you on!*

Bet this bit of information will spark a tweet—a recent survey in 2013, of 80,000 people, from all over the world, polled these results about marriage. Sit down, girls! 75% of American couples have never taken a romantic vacation. 56% of these same couples say they never kiss passionately; and 44% of American couples never go out on a date.* Got your attention now? You better check out your desperate reasons to wed; if they lean more toward the fairy tale you're in for a rude awakening. Or I should say that we're in for a rude awakening? I probably need to burn all those Harlequin romance novels leftover from adolescence. (Yes, I still have a few.) But it might take an intervention!

Girls, I wasn't going to expose the "Mrs. Smiths" I had the pleasure of working with during my lifetime. I am being facetious when I say pleasure. Of course, the following examples may not represent typical wives in America.

Look, I've never been married. But I share their profiles (I can't say stories, because you really only get a snapshot of peoples' lives) to purposely avert any longing you may have at this point to fill their shoes. I don't know if it's fair play, but that's life for you! Married folk need to stop telling all their business at work. Never really thought I would use what I learned about them. But work gossip is a gold mine. Like I said though, most of the 411 came from the wives themselves. Guess they don't have anyone to talk to outside of work. Hey, to protect their reputations (since they didn't) I won't use their real names and none of them are friends or family—so there!

First of all, single and married women psychologically go to work for totally different reasons. From what I experienced, work is a haven for them. They don't want to leave the place. Secondly, they depend heavily on the friendships that they build during working hours. Can't tell you how often I cringed from hearing information that should have only been shared off the clock. Of course, this is the only reason I am able to convey some of their misery to you. Wish I could say that most of what I heard promoted marriage. Not!

Could my version of their lives be slanted negatively? Well…they had 7.5 (out of 8.0) hours a day, five days a week to shed a different light on the subject. They didn't.

I almost hate to do this. But it's for our fraternity—we single girls! There was this one 30-something-year-old bride who loved to plan events. Y'all, I believe she got married to experience planning a wedding. Why do I say this? As soon as things got difficult with her new husband the marriage was off. That's right, within two years, maybe less, after separating, she made this statement, "Girl, maybe Johnny and I can get together and double date with other people." She may have been joking, but to dismiss something as serious as marriage so easily says a lot about her initial intent. So, girls, are you in love with the idea of the wedding? I know I am not an expert, but you don't borrow a groom for a day. You actually have to live with him after the wedding. At least, I thought that was how it worked.

Another co-worker was terrified on her wedding day and even more so when it came time to have children. She grew up in a small conservative rural community expected to do the same things that her parents had done. She didn't share any joy about her wedding day or at the birth of her two sons. Mostly fear was expressed. In fact, she said that her mother became crucial in the care of both children. But this marriage will probably last since I heard her state, "in sickness and in health," when there was a discussion about divorce. So do you feel the need to get married cuz it's expected of you? Are you putting off other life dreams to pursue the idea of marriage? Like me years ago, are you terrified of being the one left out?

Now this particular 30-something-year-old wife was just "a trip," as they say. She cussed and put down her husband openly, often, and aloud. Of course, I have heard an old wise saying that a woman should never tell another woman how good things are in her relationship, lest she get curious to find out for herself. Maybe she too knew of this wisdom. She never gave us reason to desire the attention of her man. Though she did slip up once and tell us that he was an ex-con and that she had enjoyed the fruits of his crimes before he got caught. This is no doubt a "fabulous ghetto" union that may last much longer than I think. Be careful, girls, who you choose to date; they may end up being your husband!

Another 40-something-year-old wife I worked with had several children and had raised children for other family members. I truly believe that work was her social time. I sensed from things I heard her say that she felt insignificant at home. Of course, I could be jumping to conclusions. But she always seemed to be compromising her needs for everyone else or accepting her husband's decisions about things she felt strongly about. So if you want to take a secondary role in life become a wife and mother. I have heard it said over and over again from the lips of many "Mrs. Smiths."

Finally, this example is not of a co-worker, but a "serial bride" I spoke to at work on her wedding day. At the time I was a fashion buyer for a prominent retailer in Southeastern North Carolina. I can't remember if she was embarking upon her third or fourth marriage, but she was eager to share her perspective. Speaking without shame she summed up her upcoming nuptials, "Might as well try it again, you can always get a divorce." Don't you just hate her? Here we are dreaming of finding the love of our lives and she makes marriage seem so inconsequential and fleeting. This continuous cycle of matrimony can't be fulfilling.

On the flip side of that, I have never been in the midst of married women without one of them or several of them stating that they would never do it again. Or if they had to do it again, their husband would have to be rich. Obviously, neither statement is a screaming endorsement for marriage. These examples, the "serial bride" and the regretful wives reflect the complexities of this thing we yearn for.

Y'all, I thought against bringing up the topic of violence in marriage and relationships, but then I realized that many of you may not be aware of the seriousness of the topic. These stats, more than all the other points made in this chapter should make single women pause before rushing into "marital bliss." Sorrowfully, U.S. statistics show that as least three women are killed each day by their husbands or boyfriends.* Also, one in three women at one time in their life, report either physical or sexual abuse by their spouse or significant other. The level of violence increases for women who are pregnant or in child bearing years. Disturbingly, most experts feel that there are a large number of incidents unreported.* Count your friends and family members that are married. One out of three of them has experienced or will experience some type of abuse by the supposed love of their lives. Sometime after writing this chapter, I remembered with sadness an encounter with a new neighbor whose life proved these statistics all too well. One morning, she was out walking her two dogs and we stopped to chat. I learned that she and her husband had recently moved in next door and both of them worked long hours. Soon after meeting her, I heard from one of the maintenance crew that a woman was killed in the apartment complex by her husband. I had no idea who the tenant was but later I was shocked to find out that it was the same woman I spoke to that morning. The fairy tales never ever depict life after the honeymoon. **(+IV)**

There seems to be a lot of dissatisfaction, cheating, and abuse going on in marriages. Hey, looks to me like we got our choice of poison! My advice is to enjoy the meal you're served before your timely death. Seems a bit harsh? Sorry, had to do it, girls! For our sakes, I had to take some of the glamour outta the much-coveted role of "Mrs. Smith!" Now that we have knocked "your highness" off her throne, perhaps we can stomach the "lemons," we are challenged with in our everyday lives!

Christian Sidebars

(+I) Girls, sometimes when we are feeling sorry for ourselves or suffering from bouts of rejection or failure, we forget the tenth commandment. You know, thou shalt not covet. Exodus 20:17 makes it pretty clear that we are not to desire anything that our neighbor has. Not anything! Of course, that's easier said than done living in such a secularized society. This commandment reminds me of something my mother use to say all the time, "Don't ever wish to be someone else; unless you can be a fly on the wall of their home—you have no idea what people go through!" What we really need to remember when we are feeling exiled as singles in society (as were the Israelites in Babylonia) is Jeremiah's words of comfort (29:11) which gave them an assurance from God, "For surely I know the plans I have for you…plans for your good and not disaster, to give you a future of hope." There is a method to God's seemingly madness. Today as you are in all your single glory is "as good as it gets." You can't see it cuz you're too busy gazing at your neighbor's lawn. Your grass is as green.

(+II) Rarely do we stop and consider the consequences of the things we desire and pray for, especially when we're younger. Something as simple as a good night's rest can easily be taken for granted until you can no longer experience it. Psalm 4:8 suggests that sleep should be a peaceful activity (I will lie down in peace and sleep…). So, girls, treasure your nights of quiet slumber and regard them highly because God could answer your prayer for snoring Mr. Right at any time. Until then, do not worry about anything, instead pray about everything. Tell God what you need and thank him, then you will experience peace that exceeds anything we can understand (Phil. 4:6-7).

(+III) Of course, it's pretty clear that God is repulsed by adultery. The Old Testament speaks of it often metaphorically, citing the Israelites as the offender when they chose to worship other gods. But both set of scripture verses Proverbs 6:23-33 and Matthew 5:27-30 deal with infidelity between men and women literally. Matthew restates the commandment given by God to Moses, "You shall not commit adultery" and then raises the stakes by expanding the criteria for guilt, "…anyone who even looks at a man/woman with lust has already committed adultery in his/her heart." The Proverbs verses are more graphic, but they too reflect God's distaste for the transgression. Can a man/woman scoop a flame into his/her lap and not have his clothes catch on fire? Can he/she walk on hot coals and not blister his/her feet? So it is with the man/woman who sleeps with another man/woman's husband/wife. He/she who embraces him/her will not go unpunished. So, girls, no matter what the world thinks is acceptable, it ain't alright to cheat on your spouse or to cheat with someone else who is married. Just be sure you're ready to be faithful for life when you're crying out to God for the man of your dreams. It's more complex than you think. The divorce stats prove it!

(**+IV**) We all think we know what love should look and feel like. I thought I did until Dr. Tony Evans of *The Alternative* "broke it down" for me. During my early forties I believed that God was preparing me for marriage through Tony Evans' radio ministry. I faithfully listened to his sermons every evening and many times the topics related to marriage and being single. Of course, almost a decade has passed, and I am still single, so maybe I was projecting a bit on the purpose for my encounters with his relationship wisdom. But the wonderful thing is you can test all of your relationships by his definition not just your romantic ones. I use it all the time in assessing my behavior with the people in my life. For our purposes here, I will stick to how Dr. Evans presented it. Basically, it's how to tell if ya "boo" really loves you. Before I get into his reasoning, we must look at I Corinthians 13:4-8 which invites us to reflect on love that is healthy with no dysfunction. "Love is patient; love is kind; love is not jealous or boastful or rude. It does not demand its own way; it is not irritable, and it keeps no record of being wronged. Love never gives up."

Since we live in a world far less ideal we must continue to strive to express and hopefully receive the kind of love these verses describe. Dr. Evans doesn't hold back in his sermons. He insists that we not settle for love that doesn't look like that painted by 1 Corinthians 13. Right off he states that if you are wondering after a period of time whether he loves you, you are in trouble. You see love has to be visible not just imagined. Christ visibly showed love by dying on the cross for all of humanity. This act was also <u>sacrificial</u>, the second test of true love as defined by Dr. Evans. So if ya "boo" ain't sacrificing his time and treasure (where your treasure is, there will your heart be also; Luke 12:34) it may be time to examine if he is genuine. And don't let anybody call you a gold-digga cuz you expect a man to shower you with his treasure. It's relative of course to his resources and please remember that the principle works both ways. Love is tangible as well as intangible. Thirdly, Dr. Evans stated that love must be <u>judicious</u>. God cares about how we conduct our lives and if and when we stray or make poor decisions we can be subject to his discipline (Hebrews 12:6). The love of your life as well should be willing to caution you when you are making choices that will do you harm or when your actions are simply wrong. Dr. Evans closes stating finally that love must be <u>unconditional</u>. God does not withdraw his love from us for any reason. The love of God for us through Jesus Christ is beautifully stated in Romans 8:31-39. There is nothing that can separate us from God's love. If the man in your life has conditions for showing and expressing his love for you it is time to reexamine his motives.

Chapter Two

"So You're Still Not Married?"

Y'all, after that litany of gloom, I probably just lost all of my married friends, **CLAB**. Seriously though, don't you just wanna scream N-o-o-o-o-o-o-o-o, h--- no, for the one millionth time, **"I am not married?!"** (Probably a trillion for me.) And, yes, I am guilty, of **"SWL"** single while living. So charge me—lock me up—but please stop the torture—stop asking me that question.

Girls, I have felt your pain. Got good news. The pressure eases up a bit once you turn forty. Well, maybe it's not such good news—if you're in your twenties—since you may have a couple of decades to try and justify why you are still single. And justify you must—to your family, your friends, co-workers, those of your faith, and even to strangers! Then, even after you get away from the barrage of inquiry from others, you have to deal with your own personal interrogation. Believe me, this last one can be worst. What's wrong with me? Why can't I get a man to commit to marrying me? Why do my relationships always fail? Why doesn't anybody love me? Why am I always the bridesmaid and never the bride?

Unfortunately, the assault can be never-ending. Women are bombarded by images and messages of romance and wedded bliss. You see, marriage has a powerful ally—Wall Street. Remember, billions of dollars are generated from the wedding industry alone. Likewise, other industries like jewelry, travel, real estate, automobiles, furniture, large appliances, and electronics owe their success to millions of wives. Wall Street loves marriage. In our society, mass media and its machinery work 24-7 to present romantic love and marriage as the crème de la crème of existence. Constant messages are generated via radio, television, movies, the internet, social media, billboard, and magazines that blatantly and subliminally suggest to women that if you are not married, planning to get married, or engaged, your life is worthless.

Did y'all ever see the television commercial about herpes that ended with a couple walking off hand in hand into the sunset? Herpes—surely this life crisis should provoke a need for self-reflection and time alone? Come on, girls!

And how does *The Bachelor* become the number one reality relationship show on television? Can we be more gullible? Look at how easily we are manipulated into supporting platforms that subjugate us to being such one-dimensional creatures? Marriage or desolation! Get your man or perish! And as I said before, we all tend to buy into it, including me. Cinderella, dear Cinderella...you may have done us a disservice! Maybe you should have run away from the Prince shouting, "Sorry but I've got other happily-ever-after options!"

Guess what, y'all, my momma never asked me **the** question. Surprised? Of course, she had three other children of her own and two step-children who provided her with umpteen grandchildren. I can't say that for the rest of my family or the world. During my late twenties and thirties, I dreaded large family gatherings. You know, the ones where all your grandparents, aunts, uncles, and cousins show up. Sometimes, **the** question would be the first thing they would ask when you arrived. Other times, just when you thought you had escaped—you would almost be out the door—some curious relative just had to ask, "So you're still not married?" "You do want to have children, don't you?" "Are you dating anyone seriously?" "When are we gonna meet him?" These questions asked in front of a room of onlookers feel like a series of slaps to the face. Each one delivers an emotional blow more intense than the former and finally you're depleted of what little confidence you came with.

Sadly, it is not easy recovering from the distress we experience during these encounters. Of course, there were times that I had legitimate responses to these questions, but as the years pass, coming up with answers that don't make you look like a complete human failure becomes a burdensome task. **(+I)**

Sorrowfully, y'all, there is more. You know all those weddings I mentioned earlier—over 2 million in 2010, according to the U.S. census?* Feel like you been to most of them? Wouldn't it be just as romantic if these couples would just profess their love and walk off into the sunset? Why spend all of that money to torture us poor single souls?

I know it sounds selfish—again—but there was one period of several months between my mid-20s and early 30s when I was invited to a wedding a week. I'm not exaggerating—my social network was extensive. Funny—I guess you say not extensive enough to find my own groom! Anyway, want a replay of the inquisition at these affairs? Family, friends, and strangers get a free pass to badger us with **the** question and a few more.

Still, it gets worse. Want an example of our human failure on display? The tossing of the bride's bouquet. Even if you try to hide out—anyone who knows you will call you out and expose that you are a **"swl-ler!"** As the years go by…the circle of your contemporaries catching the bouquet gets smaller and smaller—and your perceived failure becomes more and more evident—cuz you're still there—catching and not throwing the bouquet! This final act of the bride exposes the answer to **the** question so visibly that it can't help but stir up the disguised pain and anguish that we try so hard to conceal.

And so, avoiding further pain and distress becomes our goal as we navigate our everyday lives around situations that force us to rationalize—and even cover up—the fact that we are still single. (FYI, I've probably watched as many romance movies as I've read romance novels.) Actress Jennifer Aniston made a desperate attempt to hide her single status in the 1995 movie *Picture Perfect* by hiring someone to play the role of her fiancé.* In a more recent film, *Baggage Claim*, which premiered in 2013, Paula Patton solicits the help of her co-workers to assist her in finding someone to marry before the rehearsal dinner of her younger sister.*

Both movies reflect the power of external pressure to provoke single women to act irrationally. Anniston's character wanted a promotion so badly that she compromised herself to meet the unreasonable requirement. Patton wanted the approval of her mother and literally flew coast to coast in search of a suitable mate.

But I actually did not have to seek evidence from the movies to support my claim. It sometimes can be so painful—this inability to experience what others around you have. It can make you so stubborn in your pursuit to the altar and so desperate that you become senseless. For me, it cost ten years of wasted time and energy. The anxiety to get married increased during a period around my late twenties when I was afraid—terrified—that I would not find anyone else to marry beside the man I was with. And so, I invested a lot of time off and on…hoping…fantasizing that this one particular man was the right one…and I waited. I waited so long that I had to try to prove to everyone that he was the one.

Finally, after hoping for close to ten years, I had to come to grips with the fact that he was never gonna marry me! I can still remember the last date we shared and how easy it was for him to pretend that getting married was still possible. He was just humoring me. Or should I be honest and say using me as a back-up plan for his desires? After giving him an ultimatum, months later, there still was no proposal and no diamond ring. Enough was enough! I was almost forty and overcome with feelings of disappointment and grief.

Oddly enough, I realize now that I did not even love or like him. As well, I can admit that it wasn't totally his fault—some of that belongs to the pressure of getting older and remaining single. Sadly, both are still unpopular in America. You're familiar with the term, *old maid*. Guess what? The women in Japan are called "Christmas cake" if they are not married by twenty-five.* It implies that they were left on the shelf, like pastries, past their sell-by date. That just ain't right! I looked it up and found that most countries have a similar term for us—translated more often as spinster. I didn't check, but I betcha big bucks that there ain't no equivalent description for men—in any language! **(+II)**

Getting a sour taste in your mouth yet? Wish we were still bashing married life? I know…it felt so much better. It's always easier to examine other folk's troubles—their lemons. I know that the pressure has eased a bit, girls, but it still ain't easy for us to mask the panic, is it? Or to deny our greatest fear, that one day we'll wake up and the old maid will show up in our mirror. Consequently, we single girls exist between a rock and a hard place: the pressure from the world to conform and the inner turmoil that results. At times I know

that the frustration and stress of broken relationships and loneliness compel us to conduct daunting sessions with ourselves, pondering answers to **the** question, pondering what we could have, would have, and should have done. And when regret and self-doubt enter the room, you can be assured of an all-nighter; tears until dawn, self-annihilation, and exhaustion. Maybe we will even make calls to menfolk we should have long forgotten, should have never even given the time of day. Just trying to reduce the pain, repair our egos. Girls, I know you thought maybe I had forgotten, since I am fifty-something? Trust me, it's just under the surface, even though I have mastered this thing called re-imagination, making lemonade. **(+III)** I can't wait to show you how, but first more perils to examine, buckle up, the ride may still be a bit rough.

Christian Sidebars

(+I) Sorry, girls! Just like we should not covet anything as Christians, likewise we should be anxious for and about nothing (Phil 4:6-7). Both admonitions seem so absolute and obtainable. Of course, sitting around watching the dreams of others come true while you wait in the wind for yours ain't no easy task. Nor is being on constant display for others to enquire why you can't accomplish what those around you seem to do easily. Jesus let us know that we would experience trials and great sorrows (John 16:33). Of course, our victory is in the fact that he overcame the world and if we follow the example he set forth, so can we. If we humble ourselves under God's hand (I Peter 5:6-7) he will lift us in due time, so we should cast our anxiety on him because he cares for us. Though times are challenging for single women we have a comforter to call upon for solace and spiritual renewal.

(+II) As a young woman in my late twenties, I cannot say that I was pleased with the biblical wisdom that I confronted concerning living single. I was not ready to accept the fact that maybe God intended me to be single and that there was a purpose to it all. Honestly, I didn't want to hear it! It was too painful to think that I might have to live my entire life loveless and alone. Why me? I'm just being honest. But Paul explains in the letter to the Corinthians (I Corinth., Chapter 7) that the single person has more time to focus on the work of God. He states that he wishes more people would remain single (verses 6-7) and it is even better than being married (verse 38). Dr. Tony Evans had this to say in his publication *Single and Satisfied,* "*But* the time that others devote to family concerns, you can invest in kingdom-building.* That is God's plan of action for the unmarried. Undivided devotion to the Lord is the calling of every Christian and the key to being a satisfied single." I struggled a long time with this concept. Perhaps my rebellion is part of the reason I remain single. David did say in Psalm 37:4, "Delight thyself in the Lord and he will give thee the desires of your heart." (KJV)

(**+III**) Sometimes we are overwhelmed by the messages from the secularized world in which we live. To combat depressing thoughts and frustrations we must discipline ourselves to focus daily on the Word of God. We forget often that relief is just pages away. (Or an app away in these technological times.) "Your word is a lamp for my feet and a light for my path." (Psalms 119:105). (KJV)

Chapter Three

The "Terrible Thirties"

Tick…tick…tick! Yeah, we hear the clock and yes, we know most women are married by twenty-six, 26.1 to be exact, in the U.S. and we heard—guess how many times—that most doctors think it is best to have babies while you're in your twenties and preferably before late thirties.* Think we have not tried—even after being told a lot of bull- - - - like, "if it don't fit, don't force it, just relax and let it go," and "you will meet him when you least expect it" or "he's probably just around the corner"? What corner, witch? Take me to it! (I never ever lower myself to call another woman the "b" word, but you feel me.) Sound angry, don't I? Just a bit of regressing, forgive my tantrum—but "swl-ling" through your thirties—it's a bitch!

Y'all aren't tired of the references to movies, are you? Hope not—sorry, but I readily think in the context of movies because I have been a buff since adolescence. (See my filmography at the end of this book.) I got a great example for this chapter—the character Rachel could be our poster child. In the movie *Something Borrowed* from 2011, Rachel, (Ginnifer Goodwin) is just leaving her 30th surprise birthday party and she pauses as she takes a glimpse of herself in the glass window where the party was held.[*] Depressed, she states, "An old maid...I'm past my prime childbearing years...I wasted my entire twenties." **(+III)** No better dialogue could have been written for the distressed 30-something swl-ler.

Oops, I just realized that I would be remiss if I didn't pay homage to another pop culture character created by writer Helen Fielding, who gave us probably still the most famous 30-something singleton as the English would call her— Bridget Jones. Sorry about that, "Bridge!" She endeared herself to us first in the movie *Bridget Jones' Diary* in 2001.[*]

It's so twisted—a paradox. The best years biologically for major life decisions can be the years you least understand yourself psychologically. We are so much more influenced by group consensus—still so impressionable during our twenties and sometimes throughout our thirties. We're so unlikely to claim that we don't have to be like everybody else! And if you are a late bloomer like I was—embracing emotional stages later than others—then you can run out of time quickly. Tick...tick! (Of course, that is not the only reason that I remain single.) A perfect example of the power of group consensus occurred within a family of three girls from my old neighborhood. Both the first and second daughter got married and had at least one child before they finished college. The third, the youngest daughter, surprisingly, during her early teens made known her desire to pursue a career as a fashion model. For years she maintained her interest, but before long she succumbed to the pressure—she finally got engaged and had her first child too. (Check out the book *Marry Smart* by Susan Patton, A.K.A. Princeton Mom, for her take on marriage and children.[*])Personally, I was disappointed for her since she could have followed her dream and still have had time for a husband and family. Yeah, I know what y'all are thinking. She could still have a modeling career. Last I heard, she is working at a manufacturing plant. You see, girls, this is the kind of pressure we can experience from people around us as we continue to age, remain single and childless. It takes a mature, enlightened person to overcome the external pressures and inner turmoil that afflicts our existence. It is unusual for these characteristics to be fully developed in young adults, aged 18-35. Since the divorce rate in America hovers around 50%, (and higher by some sources), it is safe to suspect the wisdom of some choosing to marry.[*]

Speaking of divorce…y'all won't believe what another study had to say about 30-something swl-lers and marriage. You think we don't have enough to contend with? Remember the movie *Just Wright,* when the iconic Queen Latifah (Leslie) replies to her father's insistence that she will find someone, "I'm 35…when is it gonna happen?"[*]

According to a 2015 study by psychologist Nicholas H. Wolfinger at Utah University, if you don't get married by thirty-two it ain't gonna matter. In fact, he claims that the data concludes that if you want a successful marriage—one not ending up in divorce court—you better marry by your late twenties! He tightens the vice on the 30-something further by asserting that the chances for divorce increase every year after age thirty-two.* Talk about raising the stakes.

Sorry, I know y'all are trying not to let this inflate your desperation quotient. Guess we should have paused and asked all you 30-something swl-lers to put on a blindfold for this news. I know. The last thing you need is something more to speed up that internal clock.

Now, girls, don't go trying to lock down that man in your life like I did in Chapter Two. Guess what? I just thought of it. Stupid me…I got proposed to twice between the ages of 28-30…well…I didn't know…one of them might have worked out. Actually, this is a recent study and would not apply to me since earlier studies claimed "the older you were the better." Hey, I got out of that one!

Despite the divorce rates, women still hope the man in their lives will one day "put a ring on it," as Beyoncé demanded in her pop single.* As years go by though, it's hard to watch the dreams of others become reality over and over again. It ain't no cakewalk facing the fact that you're getting older, and that there are fewer prospects around. It's been stated that after young adulthood (18-35), the number of men to women decreases. It's probably because men have a greater willingness to risk their lives by indulging in drugs, drinking, and violent activities. I'm not whining, it's the truth; a man past his average marriageable age (28.2 in the U.S.) has a better chance of finding a suitable mate and most can have children whenever they want!* Just look at movie actor George Clooney, who at fifty-five has recently gotten married and is having twins. On top of that, women and men are still held to different standards. Single men are still not stigmatized like single women. Remember, *old maid* and *Christmas cake*? No, girls, I am not calling you names, LOL. But these terms are still being used to ostracize and degrade single women. So let me tell you how swl-ling during my thirties was for me!

It was so easy to love 'em and leave 'em when I was in my twenties. Yes, I had it like that! No…you know what I mean. Anyway, as you get older there are fewer men who will want to date or marry you. Yeah, girls, mid to late thirties—for marriage—even today a lot of folk see it as "older." Sure, you see more mature women with younger men, but this is not commonplace.

Also, as you get older, worse than not having a decent date for a long time, is the break-up with someone that you hoped would be Mr. Right. The period after the break-up can be more difficult because, as you get older, it is harder to find men you genuinely want to build lasting relationships with or ones you even like. Emotionally, this perceived failure can be draining, and it can weaken your resolve to make good dating choices. Some women become bitter as a result, and express their pain by male bashing. "Girl, I don't need no man!" Others, as time go by, begin to compromise their wish lists. Worse still is the inability for some of us to realize when we have compromised too much. Oftentimes we allow inappropriate liaisons to drag on and on. We're talk more about that later in Chapter Five.

After age thirty-five, I believe that it was hard for me to accept that another one had "bit the dust." Every time a relationship ended there was a period of great sadness and disbelief. I did not want to start all over again. I would hold on to any remnant of hope to keep from moving on. "You'll meet someone else"—words meant for solace—made me cringe.

Picking yourself up and starting again becomes a burdensome task. After these failed relationships, it is easy to feel unwanted, undesirable, and yes... old! Been there! I know... some of you are begging me to make lemonade! Not just yet. There are still some other situations that can really irritate us. No ifs, ands, or buts about it, girls...the dating game can be tough after age thirty. Man, these lemons are piling up!

When I was in my twenties, I never ever thought I would dread weekends! As we get older that party/gotta hang out feeling diminishes. At least it should. By the time I was in my mid-thirties I was looking forward to settling down. During the years earlier, I had several opportunities to pursue serious relationships. I always thought that I had all the time in the world to find a suitable mate. Before I knew it, I was 30-something and everyone else was married. I often berated myself for choosing folly over good sense in my associations with men. You see it didn't matter that I was not ready 'till then, the stats don't lie. There were fewer suitable men to choose from. I was used to always having a date, "going with someone," or hangin' out to meet someone. Man, me and the girls would hang from Thursday to Sunday. We had a ball! After age thirty, all of that begins to change.

I began to dread the weekend. Well, not the entire weekend, just Saturday! Date night. But, my attitude was different—I had no desire just to hang out,. I needed a more fulfilling connection. So I can remember reflecting on past relationships, hoping desperately that there was a potential lifelong mate among them. At wits' end, I would even reconsider men I never gave the time of day.

Sometimes I would date men again, hoping that the reasons we were incompatible had changed. This was never the case. I'm not proud of it, but I also dated guys I knew I had no interest in just to not to be alone on Saturday night. It was stupid, right? It was just one night. But it never failed; I could function all week happy-go-lucky and then the dread of Saturday would hit me. Even worse than being alone without a date was the fear that everyone would know I was dateless. God forbid anyone see me out alone on Saturday night! I was ashamed of being alone. I didn't want anyone to know that I couldn't find a date. It was like something was wrong with me. During my late thirties, my social life took a definite turn for the worse. Most of my friends were married or nursing their "piece of a relationship." To some women, a bad relationship is better than not having one!

Now, girls, let's discuss vacations, and all you Stella's trying to get your groove back!* I was never fond of taking vacations and traveling with a bunch of girlfriends. It was probably because I had three sisters, and our family shared a lot of leisure time together. And so, my idea of a perfect vacation included someone "tall, dark, and handsome," not going to search for someone tall, dark, and handsome. As you know, things didn't turn out so well for the real Stella (Terry McMillan).

I decided to be more adventurous one spring season because I hadn't taken a vacation out of my home state for a while. After several telephone conversations earlier in the year, I had re-acquainted myself with an old college friend that lived in Miami, Florida. I was curious to find out more about his personal life and though it was premature, I began having visions of us walking along the beach and dock where the cruise ships departed. So I decided to travel to Miami with one of my divorced girlfriends. I couldn't just pop up in the city alone. And no, he had no idea what my intentions were. This was my fantasy!

So there we were. That's right, Darlene and I, not Mr. Right (or Mr. Wrong) and I, walking along the Biscayne Bay. You guessed it…things didn't work out as planned. Can you imagine star-studded nights, the lighted party boats floating along in the water, the cool breeze brushing against faces, and the laughter of couples from the cafes and restaurants? As we walked along, we both knew that something was missing from the depiction above! Later, months after the trip, we laughed as we confessed that we both had similar thoughts. Though we had some fun, (it was during Cinco de Mayo) we both wished that we could have shared those nights with someone romantically. Hey, weekends and vacations can be a crap shoot for 30-something swl-lers!

You know, as the years go by, you never really imagine that you will remain single even after all the external and internal pressures you endure. You just know that one day, like all the others, you'll meet Mr. Right and all your misery will have been worth the wait. "Good things come to those who wait," right? Then out of the blue, it sort of creeps up on you and before long you're thirty-nine wondering where the time went. Of course, women still get married and have children long after their thirtieth birthday. Believe me, I got proof—I was still receiving invitations to the joyous occasions into my forties. But for many the ticking of the clock will get louder as they move toward the dreaded fortieth birthday. **Tick!!!...Tick!!!...Tick!!!**

Accompanying the incessant internal noise is the day-to-day attempt to enjoy single life. Yes...the genius at re-imagination said it: It is what it is. Though bitter as lemons. You see...you still gotta get on with life—as a swl-ler. You still gotta face each new sunrise—even though you won't like the truth it exposes. You still gotta endure the same dreaded scrutiny of family, friends, co-workers, folk of your faith, and interact within the general community— oftentimes alone. The barrage of stressors will not end. The holidays (the worst) will still exist; social job obligations, high school and college class reunions, concerts, plays, sporting events, vacations, and other social activities will drain us of creative excuses and maneuvers that we use to save face. And baby...don't forget that the inevitable weekend will always come!

I hear some of you protest: Well, it's not that bad! Sure, a lot of us start out with a support group of friends that we can hang out with. But as the years pass, that support group dwindles. And anyway, don't you get sick of inviting women to accompany you everywhere? I don't know about you, but it gets old (sorry, girls).

Sure, there are those of us who can always find a special friend or a date to ease some of the tensions of swl-ling. All of us know one woman like that. Yes...we hate her too! **JJ.** Uniquely, as swl-lers these challenges are our burden to bear. But we can't be crybabies about it, right? Having tantrums won't change our situation, will they? We gotta take the good with the lemons. Girls, no doubt... swl-ling through your thirties just ain't for sissies. Lemonade anyone? (With a splash of gin?) I know. I'm about ready for some too! **SETE.**

Christian Sidebars

(+1) I have been terrified by the passage of time since my late twenties. I enjoyed the success of my professional life, but I just couldn't get the same results personally. I was so terrified by my late thirties that I would have gotten married for the sake of marriage. I know that this is true now as I reflect back as a wiser 50-something-year-old swl-ler. I thank God that my efforts were intercepted. As I have matured spiritually and aligned my life with the will of God, I know that all things are possible, and I take comfort in Ecclesiastes 3:1-8, which promises that there is a season for all things; thus a season will come for a fulfilling personal life. I will have one last honorable love affair—one that both God and I will be pleased with.

Chapter Four

Cinderella Turns Forty

In my journal, May 26, 1999, I wrote, "The day had arrived that I always dreaded...forty...still single. I had fought a good fight...now I had to face the music...and the tune would not be 'Here Comes the Bride'."

Yes, girls, it was heartbreaking. No prince; no happily ever after. There was no 40th birthday celebration for Cinderella. Not in any of the versions I'd ever watched or read—and there were many. All my struggling—and no Harlequin romance novel ending?

I know; if I stopped to analyze things that could be part of the problem. But all I could think was that I would not get to use all those beautiful wedding plans; there would be no honeymoon filled with endless nights of passion; no one to show off to family, friends, and the world (let's just admit this desire); no birth of two baby boys (I always wanted a traditional family); no home smelling of delectable casseroles, baked goods, and fragrant candles; heck, no

diamonds! I dreaded my future—a life filled with more lonely moments and striving to exist on my own.

At forty, after being single many years, it really hits home—the realization that you didn't snag Mr. Right and that you are childless. (Of course, that's my total truth; some of you probably have children.)

But did you girls think it strange that the topic of loneliness was one that I had not yet discussed in detail? Perhaps it's because I am older and somewhat removed (genius at re-imagining) from it. Maybe cuz it is one of the more difficult areas of being single. **(+I)**

Sorry to say, it comes with the territory. No way to sugarcoat it…re-imagine it (not yet)…it's a lemon for sure. It ain't easy shaking the dread that sneaks upon you when you've spent months dateless and on your own.

Nor can you easily shake the emptiness that can be felt living day to day without that special someone to help "ease the pain of the world," (a phrase from a character created by author Alexander McCall Smith).*

And what about babies? The older I got the more sensitive the topic became. Even now at fifty-something I feel a tug at my heart when I see babies or hold them close. I used to dream about my baby boys. As time passed, the images of my possible sons faded. During my late thirties, I had Dr. Cooper, my gynecologist, to check the viability of my eggs. I was still able to have a child of my own.

Later, Dr. Cooper insisted that I could still carry a child to term even if my eggs were not viable. In excitement, he let me know that, as a fertility specialist, he performed the procedure all the time. I could take an egg from one of my nieces (they are some productive girls) and have it fertilized by the man of my choice...LOL.

Guess what, I do have a niece that looks a lot like me; my younger brother's oldest child. It just didn't appeal. Dr. Cooper said that I should decide soon...time slipped away...still wanted my dream to come true...the package (hubby and baby)...

I waited too late. Yeah, I hear you! Of course, I could still adopt or foster children. Regrettably, I am an all or nothing kind of girl!

Thank goodness for nieces and nephews. Got a bunch! But I still won't experience something I feel folk with children may take for granted; the intimacy between child and mother. I have a niece who is like a daughter to me, but one evening I was made painfully aware that many times aunties can't substitute for mommie. My niece, I think she was nineteen at the time, came home upset after hanging out with friends. I could hear her explaining to her mother what had happened. I wanted to chime in and console her, but as I stepped toward the door of the bedroom I could see her curled up beside her mother on the bed. It was not a moment for aunties to intervene. I walked away knowing that I would probably never experience that level of intimacy with a child. It hurt, even though I am so grateful for the relationships that I have with all my nieces and nephews. More anxiety. Like I said earlier, it comes with the territory.

Now, girls, I ain't gonna lie to you; the 40-something and older swl-ler got a lotta other burdens to bare. **(+II)**

Unfortunately, as the years pass she will have to adjust to being almost invisible as a candidate for marriage.

Yeah, they say that today's forty is really like being thirty! All my forty-year-old single friends are having a heck of a time proving this. Have you heard the Oscar-winning song "It's Hard Out Here for a Pimp"?* Just insert single forty-year-old women where appropriate!

We have to live with everybody's assumption that there's little hope…that we will probably never wed or have children. Everybody else is married; So you often get to share with friends only if their menfolk got plans with the boys— you're just a Plan B.

"Let me check with Harry." This is the married friend's theme song.

No, I am not hating! LOL. Every weekend becomes challenging—negotiating your social life through married family and friends. But you do get to acquire a new role as babysitter since you obviously have no plans on the weekends. Then there are the dreaded blind dates or getting "fixed up" for social occasions that many single women suffer through.

Personally, I have few stories to share about the subject. Perhaps it's because after college I moved back home to a smaller metropolitan city. When you reside in an area throughout adulthood single usually there aren't many men left to be "fixed up" with. Oops, I forgot, there was one occasion, yeah, a much shorter guy (yes, I have issues with that too, like a lotta y'all). Needless to say it was fruitless— since I am writing this book.

Even nursery rhymes from our childhood endorse the idea that a woman needs a man in her life. Remember, "Jack and Jill went up the hill to fetch a pail of water."* Did she really need Jack to fetch the water? I digress. Unwillingly the 40-something-year old-swl-ler is forced to become Jack, that is "jack of all trades," and she's often ashamed (at least I was) of not having someone to do what I call "**man chores**." I know that sounds sexist. Of course, I know married women who end up performing their own "man chores," but for some reason family members and friends are less sympathetic to us swl-lers.

Y'all, it takes me a while to come up with the nerve to ask for help and when I do, I still feel like a failure for not having my own man to assist me. Once I moved almost completely on my own. (I did hire movers for all the really heavy stuff.) The family member who did help didn't waste an opportunity to remind me of my status. "Girl, you haven't found yourself a man yet?"

And there was the time that I rode around with a new television in my car for months because it was too heavy for me to carry inside my apartment. I can hear you say, "Girl, you crazy!" I tell you, it's the shame that gets you. But check this out! When I finally asked a neighbor's fiancé to discard the old television, you wouldn't believe the look of superiority she had as he lifted it out and took it to the dumpster. Her man! That's the reaction I was trying to avoid. (Of course my perception of their kind gesture may have been twisted, since they parted later and probably were just roommates living together through tough times.)

Worse still was the year I dug myself out of a snowstorm during Christmas time to get to the rest of the family. And don't let there be an issue with my car. Hate it! Yes…that's right…I guess I do believe that some things are just for men to handle. You know women get ripped off every day if they are alone seeking help with car repairs.

Over the years the list of other inconveniences has grown: no one to turn the mattress as recommended, no one to help with those dresses that are hard to zip up, no one to scratch your back in those unreachable spots, no one to massage away the stress of a long day, and no one to go out in the cold and scrape the frost from your car windows. (I hear you. I am too old school!)

One morning, before work, I cried because I couldn't get the top off the coolant fluid. It was early, cold and I finally had to suck it up and wake a neighbor to get it off. Girls, I know…you wanna ask if I'd like cheese with all that whine. But can't y'all just admit that there are some things we need men for?

Speaking of…there's also the lack of intimacy, physical and emotional, over periods of time that compound the stress for the 40-something and older swl-ler. One scene in the movie *Hitch* sums up this distress beautifully.* Will Smith's character crashes a speed dating event by holding up the process to speak to Eva Mendes. Before long, an older female participant screams out, "Can we move this along? I haven't got laid in 6 months!" (I may be paraphrasing a bit.) She may be one of the lucky ones, since it was only six months. Personally, I see having sex today as a live or die undertaking. **(+III)**

You know we are not living in those periods of supposed low-risk, fun-loving sexual activity. I am not joking when I say to you girls that "You need to see papers clearing folk of all diseases." Sex may be great, but it ain't worth dying for! I hear some of you saying, "Speak for yourself." Naughty…naughty! (Chapter Ten covers more of this discussion.) I don't agree with medical assertions that women peak sexually around their mid-thirties. I've discovered that the 40-something swl-ler is still fighting a heightened sexual desire (I know from my experience and from what other women friends have shared) that started during their late thirties. I say fighting because the 40-something swl-ler may find herself doing what I call "entertaining strangers" (dating men they would normally not give the time of day) for the sake of intimacy. Submitting to any one of the big three tempters (we will get to them in Chapter Five) can create a dangerous liaison that could last well beyond what the swl-ler intended.

On top of all of this, 40-something and older swl-lers may be accused of having certain undesirable traits. Yes…we have lived on our own for some years. Yes, we have "one less egg to fry," a phrase from a song written by Burt Bacharach in 1970.* (I know most of you are too young to remember it. Does Fifth Dimension ring a bell? No. Anyway. It just sounded good to use it at this point.)

Yes…we get to enjoy that wonderful space at home all to ourselves. That's right…we cook when we want or not...the room temperature is changed how and when we desire...our standard of housekeeping becomes law...we spend our money how and when we like, and no one monitors our comings and goings. Does any of this automatically make us selfish or self-absorbed? Hey, it's like I said in Chapter Three, it ain't like we didn't try to get married.

And no...I cannot hide my independence or the unintentional message it sends that "I don't need a man." I was just having a conversation with my nephew when he shocked me with, "Auntie, you don't even need a man."

So I easily throw up the hood to a car and know how to top off most of its fluids. Didn't I just say how much I hated doing these "man chores?" Yes...I have lived on my own and financially provided for myself for many years (sometimes with help) through economic recessions and good times. And yes, I travel wherever I want, anywhere I want often alone.

So what's so wrong with being self-sufficient? Why is it such a dirty word? Why are men that you meet and date intimidated by this trait? Yes...they are, girls! Some of you have yet to learn this. Don't be fooled into believing that they are forward-thinking (well...most are not) or enlightened. On average they are still cavemen. Hey, it's too late in the game for being frail and dying our hair blonde. (Sorry...I should be ashamed to use such a stereotype.) We gotta deal with the lemons we get. Shoot, y'all, the 40-something swller just can't get a break. She's damned if she does and damned if she doesn't! Boy, all that venting felt good!

Don't you hate all the hoo-rah about turning forty? Now we got to replace our "how to getta man" manuals with some more bull- - - - from *O Magazine* and others like it (sorry, Oprah) touting the wonders of the magical age and its liberating powers. Makes me wanna holla and throw a "terrible thirties" tantrum!

Can we first acknowledge the pain from possibly ten to twenty years of disappointment before we celebrate our apparent glorious fourth decade? Can we be honest about how we really feel? Do the folk who endorse this magical passage of life care to know that it's as if my existence as a viable mate has evaporated? Do they know that no one gives a- - - - (insert your own four "4" letter word) whether I got married or not…or that I feel defeated…impotent…and that can be worse than loneliness. Don't they get that all my education… accomplishments…work…service to the community is diminished…rendered insignificant…when I am asked **the** new question: "So…you **never** got married, did you?" Like a death sentence.

Making too big a fuss about nothing, you say? Liz Tuccillo, co-author of *He's Just Not into You*, may disagree with you. She was in her early forties when the book became a bestseller. This short passage from the book depicts the anguish that most swl-lers experience at some point if we're honest enough to admit it: "…I don't know about you, but I hate being single. I hate going to parties alone. I hate sleeping alone. I hate waking up alone. I hate knowing that every single boring errand I have to do, I'm going to do alone. I hate not having sex. I hate looking for one and shopping for one. I hate going to weddings. I hate people asking me why I still am single. I hate people not asking me why I am still single…"* **(+IV)**

Girls, I'm sure Liz and I, like all the millions of other women who dreamed of meeting their knight in shining armor who at the last moment rides in and rescues them from a life of obscurity, never imagined that we were gonna become that "lady," the 40-something swl-ler; that lady in every community that everybody wonders about.

Why didn't she get married? What's wrong with her? (Asked while raising one eyebrow.) Or imagined that we would experience embarrassing interrogations from strangers, like the one at my favorite restaurant for carry-out, "Why don't I ever see you with a man?" Painful encounters, no, actually, brutal would be a more accurate description.

Time has passed…but some things have not changed…desire the same…still the same at 50-something… it's not easier to take…I am not tougher…life comes full circle.

I myself had asked the same questions about older single women when I was younger. I was reminded of the "bag lady," a homeless woman from my old neighborhood. The story was told that she had a mental breakdown after the love of her life abandoned her. Perhaps she too had waited years, through her twenties and thirties to meet someone and at long last thought her dreams were coming true. Instead, she had to come to grips yet again with the fact that her dreams would be denied. Maybe she too had celebrated her fortieth birthday, still single, and it was hard to face a possible future with no prince and no happily ever after. **(+V)**

"Sniff, sniff," I need some tissue. I'm not being funny. Man…if this isn't a perfect time to flip this script. Just one more chapter, girls, and these sour realities will be history!

Oops—left out one other issue that the forty-something single women may have to add to their list of angst as she gets older and closer to retirement. Hate to do it! Hate to add another check in the positive column for married women. AARP reports in a recent book advising single women about retiring that the average income for single women in our country is around $27,000.*

$27,000? I have been working so hard to create quality life for myself and it ain't easy to acknowledge that financially I may have gained more wealth as a married woman. You see, men still have and make more money than women. Pastor Stenneth Powell in his inspiring marriage guide, *What to Do Before You Say "I Do"* confirms my fears when he writes that one of the purposes of marriage is to acquire wealth.*

And so, girls, must we also struggle with our net worth? No "honey" or money! Heck, I am gonna need that lemonade—now—doused with gin!

Christian Sidebars

(**+I**) It usually takes great effort to distinguish between loneliness and being alone. But the line drawn is easily blurred for the swl-ler the longer she remains single. In my early twenties, I would never have imagined that I would be alone through my 30s, and 40s. And I never would have imagined the feelings of loneliness that I would have to overcome to fully enjoy life. I would come to rely totally on my faith to make this transition. God promises that he will never leave or forsake us in Hebrews 13:5. God became my refuge and my strength through the years as promised in Psalm 46:7. Today, my family and friends can hardly believe how much I enjoy my time alone. You could say that God helped me to perfect the art of being alone.

(**+II**) If you remain single for many years, there will be occasions during your single journey when you will not be able to escape the perils of having become a mature single woman. There will just be days that you will dread being you. Being recognized as an alone, single woman many years past the average marrying age and unlikely to bear children won't be amongst your finest hours. Thankfully, these verses found in II Corinthians 4:8-11 respond to the despair we may encounter as we grow older and remain single: "We are pressed on every side, but we are not crushed, we are perplexed but not driven to despair; we get knocked down, but we are not destroyed." Because Christ suffered, died, and rose again we can experience the same victory. Remember, "Trouble don't last always." This too shall pass!

(+III) I made a foolish statement as a young woman that I would have to painfully retract. A good friend and I were just in disbelief that God actually wanted us to be virgins on our wedding night. We actually made jokes about it. Years later, after communing with God through scripture, prayer, and song I was able to discipline myself to live celibate for long periods of time. Oftentimes we want to set aside a part of our lives to God's sovereignty. As we mature spiritually we realize that God's statutes and principles are for our own good. Sharing ourselves sexually with various partners who "hump and dump" (sorry to be so harsh) us can be emotionally painful and degrading.* Dr. Tony Evans reminds us of our responsibility as single believers. Dr. Evans believes that the Bible assumes that if you are single, you ought to be a virgin, either physically or by virtue of your relationship with Jesus Christ. Remember, whoever is in Christ is a new person. You no longer live for yourself, but for Christ's sake (2 Corinthians 5:17). Since the topic of sexual abstinence is so challenging for the Christian single I thought it only fair to present another viewpoint; Rev. Dr. Susan Newman provides an interesting one for all of us in her book, *A Black Woman's Guide to Sex and Spirituality* (ISBN 0345450779). Her stance on celibacy and the Christian journey is enlightening.

(+IV) Jesus stated, "I have come that you might have life and have it more abundantly." (John 10:10, KJV) If you didn't know it by now it should be obvious that I live by the promise of this scripture. Of course, by the time I turned forty still single God would have had to renew my strength and resolve many times over. For me, becoming forty and still single offered no crown of glory. Thankfully, our faith develops life producing traits like love, joy, resilience, and patience. These fruits of our faith help us live as Paul stated in Phil 4:11, "for I have learned to be content with whatever I have." (KJV)

(+V) Job knew well the grief that great disappointment and heartbreak can bring. As we get older and remain single we too have experiences that leave us broken and hopeless. Sometimes like Job 7:11, "we cannot keep from speaking; we must express our anguish, our souls must complain." The hurt from broken relationships can be overwhelming and debilitating, sometimes to extreme ends. Hopefully even in our pain we continue to commune with God so that we can be comforted by the words from Isaiah 40:31, "but those who wait on the Lord shall renew their strength, they shall mount up with wings like eagles, they shall run and not be weary, they shall walk and not faint." As a 50-something Christian single I can assure you that if you just hold on to your faith that you will experience the restoration promised above.

Chapter Five

Waiting to Exhale!

Monica (Sanaa Lathan), challenges Quincy (Omar Epps), to a one-on-one basketball game for his heart. Confidently, she makes this challenge the night before his marriage to another woman. As the game begins it appears as if Monica is going to win. However, Quincy decides to pick his game up and he gets to 5 points first, winning. As she turns away from him, head hung in defeat, he relents. As she hugs him with tears streaming down her face in relief—she exhales!

This scene from the movie *Love and Basketball* is a classic example of what every woman desires.* Getting her man! When Monica exhaled, she released all the pent-up frustrations and expectations of millions of women everywhere. I know...a bit dramatic...but that's what it felt like.

But it was just another adaptation of Cinderella. Remember when the shoe fit...can't you just hear the air escape her lungs?

Girls, we just can't seem to get away from the fairy tales or our preoccupation with falling in love or finding the man of our dreams.

Since adolescence, my siblings have accused me of being in love with love and the love story. Like I said earlier, they would watch me swoon over romantic comedies or ridicule me for always being curled up in my room reading Harlequin romance novels. This preoccupation may or may not have anything to do with reasons why my relationships never evolved into marriage.

In my defense, recent figures show that romance literature generates 1.4 billion dollars in revenue, the largest category for the entire literary industry.[*] To my surprise, though, the average age for readers, forty-five, is years older than I was when I began to read the novels. So maybe I do need to admit that this medium had a lot to do with shaping my perception of love and relationships. At forty-five, the readers are probably married and just trying to escape their day to day unromantic lives.

But still, it's not just me. In the movie, (here I go again) *The Mirror Has Two Faces*, Barbra Streisand (Rose Morgan), a literature professor, explores why we still hope to fall in love, despite all the trouble and heartache it brings: "Because while it lasts, it feels -uckin great!"[*] And Natalie Cole, who's one of my favorites, expounds on the topic as well on her jazz album *Ask a Woman Who Knows* by singing that love is "Better Than Anything."[*]

Girls, I don't know why I am defending my preoccupation with love—it isn't always the reason that women marry. **(+I)**

Oops, did I let the cat out of the bag?! Y'all know some of the other reasons. Y'all know the truth behind some of the nuptials: societal/family pressure, security/wealth, to start a family, already pregnant…and don't forget some women are simply "on the rebound."

As I look back, I realize that there was another distinct moment during my twenties that would influence my future relationship choices. On my first job out of college I worked with an older woman who got married to spite a former lover. During one conversation, she stressed strongly to me that if I married someone I didn't love, it would be the worst thing imaginable. I never forgot that advice and subconsciously vowed to never let it happen to me. So, armed with a bit of an unrealistic idea of love and this vow, I went forth hoping to find the man of my dreams.

Girls, listen up now. I am about to reveal my back story. If I am honest, I did find one man I would have married without hesitation. Even as I make this statement, I pause, because I know folks will say "you can have more than one love."

Sure. There were others…I'm not saying that there wasn't anyone else that I may have been moderately happy with. But I believe that people equivocate when they make the statement that "there are more fish in the sea." It hurts less than admitting that you will never ever feel that way about another person—ever. (Well, I haven't yet.) And, yeah, we could have a debate about the actual meaning of true love. But I can be away from this man for years—and even at 50-something, I can be in a room with him and know where he is every moment—feeling his presence. Feeling exactly what I felt so many years ago. I am not gonna say that true love is rare—in my opinion, what's really rare is mutual, sustaining love. And so, I know that other women have married men who were not their first choice—and whom they did not love. I guess for the reasons mentioned earlier, I was not able to do the same. Some of these marriages last. I know women who confess that they chose practically but eventually fell in love with their spouse.

Susan Patton, in her book *Marry Smart*, suggests that we be less picky choosing our spouses, especially if we have a great desire to have children.* I wanted it all—perhaps unrealistically so. I was just not willing to risk marrying someone that I wasn't passionate about.

The love of my life chose to marry someone else. From that point on, it's clear that I subconsciously compared the way I felt about him to every other relationship. I was always searching for more. And of course…time waits for no one…tick…tick. Unrequited love…what a lemon!!

Now, y'all better not feel sorry for me…it happens to the best of us. Besides I had other life passions (learn about them in Chapter Seven) and I started to have a lot of fun just having platonic interactions with men—and of course you know that women are not supposed to have any fun in their relationships—that's just for the boys! **(+II)**

Somewhere along the way…as I got older and the pressure of remaining single began to bear down…the fun stopped. But not before I got some manly advice from some fellows and warnings from others. I know y'all want me to give you more details about the fun I had—yes, I got stories…tall tales…literally, LOL, but this is not a tell all…y'all just nosy! It wouldn't help you get them to the altar…remember I am not an expert in getting and keeping a man…my genius is in being single…the ability to re-imagine…hopefully some of this advice will help you navigate your interactions with men.

After what I call my failure to "get my man" I became almost fanatic in trying to understand the species from Mars.* I read all the books expounding on the subject; I sought advice from older experienced women and I was always eager to lend an ear to my subject when he felt the need to "lay down" some wisdom about relationships. Below is my list of what I call "**lemonisms**." The first group contains advice from men extrapolated from my conversations and eavesdropping over the years; the latter are wise words from women who wish "they knew then what they know now."

Honestly, over the years neither list has brought me much comfort; more so they taunt me. Just a whole bunch of lemons!—reminders of my lack of savvy and ongoing dismay when it comes to snagging Mr. Right.

Wisdom from Men

Always have a Plan B when single and dating.
– D.T.

A man's main goal in life is not to get married—
he just gets caught.
– W. Dykes.

Attraction is important—this is someone
you will have to wake up with every morning.
– K.W.

If you are smart, you'll get clever at propping up
the male ego.
– Dr. T. Evans.

Love ain't going nowhere...
concentrate on developing yourself.
– J. Stanfield.

Men and women marry for different reasons.
– T. Agnew.

Men definitely are not looking for wives
Saturday night at the bar/club.
– Unknown

Men do not bond as quickly as women do
in relationships.
– J. Gause

Never pop in to see a man without his knowledge.
– Unknown

Relationships are like the weather—
sometimes it's stormy.
– Unknown

Wisdom from Women

A man chases a woman until she catches him.
– N. Miller

A man is motivated by only two things...food and sex.
– T. Kennedy

Don't reveal too much of yourself quickly,
emotionally, or physically.
– R. Ross

If he hits you once, it's his fault,
the second time he hits you it's yours.
– D. Carroll

If you compromise all your standards, what's left of you? –
D. A.

Listen to what he says…but watch what he does,
"talk is cheap!"
– D. A.

Love/Risk, they are synonyms.
– Unknown

Never ever marry a man you don't love.
– C. M.

Women can't think well while lying on their backs.
– Unknown

You can't get rid of a man who really cares for you.
– my momma

Girls, I guess you wore me down. I'll share an anecdote or two just to illustrate the "lemonisms" above. You didn't have to beg! I remember when I first heard one of them…like yesterday.

At twenty-four, I had one of the most incredible weekends of my life. At this point, I still had little experience dating and I realize now even less with love…real love. It just happens. You can say it is infatuation, lust…but I know marriages that last from a similar inception. Oh, if it had only been a mutual revelation. At the time he was living forty-five minutes away. Naïve, I thought it would be ok to travel and surprise him. I still remember my disbelief…how could what I felt be so one-sided? How could he be re-enacting my weekend with someone else? His close friend was the bearer of the bad news. He was unavailable to see me…he had company. Company? Then he said it, "When you're single, it's a good idea to have a Plan B." As simple as that. Crushing the life out of me…there was no other plan! It was too late. **(+III)**

That prior weekend…it happened so quickly…from the sound of his voice….to the pulsing muscles in his thighs as he shifted gears and drove us away…his confidence…his competence at wooing…all too seductive. Sorry, girls…this ain't a romance novel…that's the end of that reverie. Two hard lessons learned!

Y'all, I credit my mother with this next "lemonism" lesson. Truth is, if you're 20-something…there's probably something you've yet to learn. Mothers are always right! We hate it…but they "been there, done that."

There once was a man who told me that he lost his heart to me in the sixth grade. He remembers what I wore and the bookbag I carried. The very fact that he was so honest and real about his feelings is a rare thing. In 2012, Michelle Obama states in *Essence* magazine one of the reasons she fell in love with the President was this attribute—his authenticity.* Makes me think something is wrong with me. I dated him off and on after I finished college. Do we really know why we fall instantly one weekend for one and never can with another, after dating them for years? I tried. I mean I really tried. He was a good friend, an interesting man…we traveled…we talked for hours…we laughed (so important) and I never saw him as my husband. He asked. I liked him…maybe loved him…but not enough. (Remember the vow I made to myself?)

He married two other women. And still he pursued me into my forties. My momma always used to say, "If you worried whether a man loves you (doubting him and wondering where he is every second)…he probably doesn't…cuz you can't get rid of a man who really cares about you."

That's it, girls…just two stories…this ain't about my romances…it's about re-imagination, making lemonade…if we can get to it!

Finally, one last lemon or, I should say, group of lemons. In Chapter Four, I mentioned that the 40-something and older swl-ler may find herself "entertaining strangers." It's a sensitive time for us. The availability of eligible men has decreased, and everyone around us is married with children. Some of us may be experiencing residual heightened sexual desire from our mid-to-late-thirties. Some folk are speculating why this is our fate and it's as if we have a bull's-eye on our back for certain predators. I call them the "big three" tempters since they test our will to wait for relationships we truly desire. If we entertain these liaisons it reflects the depth of our desperation cuz they usually add very little value to our lives.

Of course, there are always exceptions to the rules. Unguarded, the 40-something swl-ler may not be conscious of her vulnerability in these situations. I hear you asking, girls...who are these culprits? After one failed relationship after another, the swl-ler sometimes develops what I call **rejection fatigue**. She gets tired of waiting around for the ideal "one," so she is prone to compromise when she least expects it. And when she lowers her standards...she can become putty in the hands of the big three. Demi Moore and Terri MacMillan, (*Stella Got Her Groove Back*) fell prey their second time around to one of the predators. Halle Berry was blessed with a daughter, but ended up paying for her involvement with another of them. And the women who Mel Gibson, Kevin Costner, and Michael Douglas traded their first wives for dealt with the worst of three.

Have you guessed who the perps are? Alright, I will tell you. First, the young man, looking to build his credibility and increase his prowess; next, the freeloader, looking to be taken care of, and last, the married man looking for that lost "lovin' feeling" or looking to revive his "player card."[*]

All three predators think that you're desperate. In fact...they are banking on it! It's truly their only way in. In normal circumstances...you would not give them the time of day. Just as the man noticed that I was rarely with a companion at the restaurant...others observe our swl-ling status; especially if we have been single for years. Since you may often be alone they think you will welcome their attention. They start out subtlety, but if you prove them right during any of their encounters, their subsequent advances grow more aggressive, so watch out, girls! Shut them down from the beginning. If you can. You see, you are human and sometimes after we have had one of those emotional meltdowns I mentioned, or if our hormones are raging, we may falter. It's understandable, but it can lead to a dangerous liaison that lasts much longer than it should. You could find yourself "loving who you with," (accepting second/third best) instead of waiting for the man of your dreams. **(+IV)**

Surprisingly, the most cunning of the three is the married man. Some may hide the fact initially, but most are bold. This predator is so aggressive that you should never give him the impression that you might be interested. Run, literally! Of course, this may excite him. I don't know what these men are missing in their marriages, but that's not your problem. If you get yourself tangled up in this threesome you deserve what you get. **(+V)** If you entertain the idea of being the other woman for any length of time, you could be headed for emotional trouble. Sorry, girls. Read my lips…"Married men are not looking for wives…they already have one."

There is an old riddle about drug addicts. How can you tell that an addict is lying? His lips are moving. Same thing applies to the married man. Delude yourself if you wanna…it's a dead end. Of course, some of us prefer dead ends—relationships with no commitment. (That's a subject for another book or your psychologist.)

Perhaps I should not have mentioned the pop culture examples earlier, since these are not average men, and all three left their wives to pursue relationships with "the other woman." Very few average "Joes" can afford to take care of two families like the movie stars mentioned were forced to do.

Now the freeloader is not as easy to identify. You could go on a few dates with this culprit before discovering his true nature. But before long, his visions of your role in his life is revealed. He speaks too soon about moving into your cozy home or apartment. You may later find out that he is unemployed and has been sleeping on the couch of some relative, "trying to get his life together." He may drop by at dinner time wondering what you're cooking. And soon...you will be paying for the dates and driving him around in your car. Also, you may discover that this perp is an ex-con, a drug addict, or just simply a lazy s-o-b! (Excuse my language).

I probably had the most fun avoiding the advances of the younger man. Very few are savvy at their attempts to woo. However, they can be persistent. I have to be honest...one got through...but earlier when I was in my late twenties.

This perp, from my experience, just wants to look good with the boys. He wants to say that he was able "to bag" (hate that phrase) an older, socially visible, sophisticated woman. Most often his attention span is short, and the demands of a serious relationship will have him looking for something shinier, sooner than later. I must add that the big three tempters don't have discriminating taste. Although 40-something and older swl-lers may be most vulnerable to them, other swl-lers need to keep their radar poised for them too!

Girls, these are the last of the lemons…I know some of you got "stuff" you could add to the list. Maybe one day soon I will get to hear about them.

There you have it; the bitter truth, no chaser! Right from the beginning, I have tried to be as candid as possible in revealing the pitfalls of living single, swl-ling. I was determined not to sugarcoat our experience. I know you…I am you, past and present! Of course, my viewpoint has been influenced by many variables. I am from a different era than most of you that I am writing to—20-40-something-year-old swl-lers, though I gladly commiserate with my contemporaries too.

Also, I am writing in an era that offers women phenomenal choices for creating quality lives, and, thankfully, the stigma of remaining single has lost some of its sting. But some things have not changed. Little girls are still immersed in fairy tales, like Cinderella, that breed adult women who long for their Prince Charming.

Not too long ago, in 2013, the Disney movie *Frozen*, merely an adaptation of Cinderella and other fairy tales like it, became the highest grossing animated film of all time.* Undoubtedly, women still prefer to get married and have families despite their careers and the strides we have made in the world. The billion-dollar wedding industry is a strong indicator of this amongst many other factors I discussed.

So many single women will have their dreams realized, but many will not. Those of us remaining single for years will feel ostracized by a culture that promotes and oft times glorify marriage. We will suffer bouts of loneliness, unworthiness, and rejection. But these are only the lemons of our experience. Only half the story. Hopefully, the stage has been set to introduce my concept of re-imagination. You see that's all lemonade is—a new state of being for the sour lemon. I'm elated—no, ecstatic, to share with you my strategy for creating an enhanced state of living even with all the pains, sorrow, and inconveniences of swl-ling. **(+VI)**

In the next section, "From Bitter to Sweet," get ready to drastically alter your view of life and what it has to offer. Girls, we 'bout to get our lemonade on! What's your pleasure...peach...blueberry...a splash of gin, anyone? Yes please...on the rocks!

Christian Sidebars

(**+I**) Believers are more comfortable separating erotic, romantic love from faith and spirituality. As ever, God is wiser as evidenced by the inclusion of the Song of Solomon in the Old Testament. This book depicts graphic erotic love that would make any of us blush (Song of Solomon, chapters 5 and 7). Romantic love is an inescapable characteristic of human life. At its best, it is life giving and strengthening. At its worse, well we all could share a story or two of its devastation. But we should never feel embarrassed or at fault for desiring or seeking it for our lives. Most times, like the late great R&B virtuoso Barry White alludes to in one of his songs, it finds you!

(**+II**) If you are not a virgin, when you accept Christ as your Lord and Savior, it is not the easiest task to begin living celibate. Once I made the commitment to God, grace and mercy allowed me to become stronger in my resolve. It is a process, like all spiritual growth. But we must try to run, literally from sexual sin (I Cor. 6:18) and God will assist us by providing an escape (I Cor. 10:13). Believe me, it occurs; there were times that I escaped by the hair of my chinny chin, chin!

(**+III**) The crushing blow of unrequited love can leave lifelong scars. We are admonished in Psalms 118:8 not to put our faith in mankind but in the Lord. 'Wish these words made it easier. 'Wish I could say after reading those and many more that the pain instantly disappeared. I can say without faltering though that, "The Lord is close to the brokenhearted and he rescues those whose spirits are crushed (Psalms 34: 18)." One glorious morning restoration will shine brightly upon you. You can bank on it!

(+IV) Temptation is as common to the Christian journey as the need to pray. The moment you confess Christ evil lurks at your door. As you grow, the greater your commitment becomes the greater the onslaught from temptation. So don't be surprised, because that which you experience is no different from what others confront. As I stated, just above, God will show you a way out so that you won't give in to it (I Cor. 10:13).

(+V) If you need a reminder on how our faith views adultery, review the sidebar in Chapter One **(+IV)**.

(+VI) The Christian journey is a unique experience characterized by many paradoxes. We are to welcome insults, hardships, and persecutions if Christ will be edified. For God is made strong in our weaknesses (2 Cor. 12:8-10). Consequently, all things work together for our good for those of us called according to God's purpose (Romans 8:28). (KJV)

Part II
From Bitter To Sweet

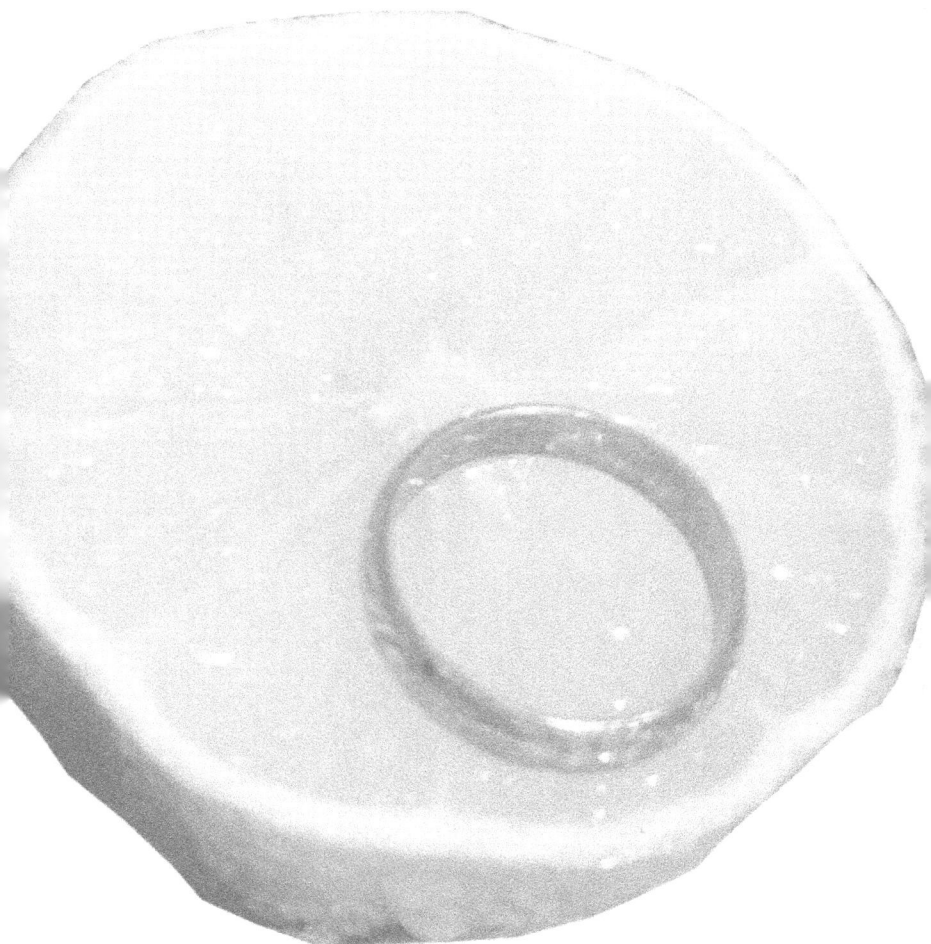

Chapter Six

Radical Gratitude

I know I said we would get right to enjoying that lemonade, soon, soon! First, I want you to understand that even though Part II of this book is supposed to "flip the script," turn lemons into lemonade, from time to time we will still need to examine some of the underlying factors that contribute to the dissatisfaction and anxiety experienced by single women.

Let's take a look at an activity that most of us engaged in as young girls. When did you start reading fairy tales? You know the romantic ones, like *Snow White*, *Sleeping Beauty*, *Rapunzel*, and the iconic *Cinderella*. Some would disagree with my classification, since they are usually grouped by the moral of each story—what it teaches the reader.*

What-evvvver! The facts cannot be disputed, as young girls we "cut our teeth" on these romantic fables promising happiness forever if we hook the prince, or if he rescues us from the evils of the world. By the time we're adults, our minds have been infused with this manipulative notion a thousand times over. (Remember, Wall Street loves marriage and romantic love.)

I think we just fail to realize the persuasiveness of these tales. Girls, can we talk about propaganda? (Did you know that most of the classic fairy tales were created and written by men?) The message of the "Cinderella" story and all of its derivatives has a lasting effect.

Even now in the twenty-first century, as I stated in Part I the onslaught continues. The 2013 movie *Frozen*, a story about sisters of royalty, is just another serving of the same dish, even though no one ends up with the prince. Trust me, someone ends up with a prospective mate and the happily ever after storyline prevails. This film became the highest grossing animated film of all time.[*] To pull this off, it had to not only have the support of new romantic fairy tale converts (female children), but thousands of ready-made disciples (female adults) programmed from childhood to tout its glory. Even I, though objective enough to make these observations, have been under the influence of the "Cinderella" story most of my life, and possibly even suffered an overdose with all the Harlequin romance novels, I read, LOL!

So what's my point? I believe that the euphoria created by fairy tales and the constant reinforcement of the narratives throughout our lives is a major contributor to our dissatisfaction with being single. You see, we develop the need to reenact the "Cinderella" storyline—find our prince, get married, and live happily ever after. The vast majority of us, and the recent survey of college students proves it, wait longingly for this moment to occur in our lives. Of course, for various reasons, millions of us may never experience this outcome. (**+I**) (Sorry, girls)!

The million-dollar question is, "How do we begin to fill such a void, if we marry much later (average age in U.S. 26.1) or never?" You see, we can't avoid the deluge of images or the moments experienced by those around us...the love affair, the long-awaited proposal, the diamond ring, the engagement party, the wedding gown, the wedding plans, the bridal showers, the wedding day, the honeymoon—their very own fairy tale! After experiencing this series of events over and over again for others and never for yourself you could easily become distraught and dejected. Y'all, there was one month during my twenties that I was invited to seven weddings. Of course, when you are in your twenties you don't doubt that your day of rapture will soon come too.

So, after many years, how did I rise above the hype? We know from Chapter One that truly that's all the above series of events represent. However, as the years pass, and you have bought one too many wedding and shower gifts, something about you changes. You begin to question your worth and your ability to actualize this dream; and then you begin having the emotional meltdowns I mentioned in Part I, Chapter One.

I believe that we are all searching for passion in our lives. We want to feel strongly, and experience things that seem larger than life. Case in point—fairy tales, or the euphoria that they embody. I think it also explains why we are so fixated on the lives and marriages of pop culture stars. Consequently, we wait around for something fantastic to happen and fail to appreciate the significance of less dramatic incidents that occur all the time.

One summer night, when I was in my mid-thirties, I had an epiphany as I sat alone on the front porch of my duplex apartment; I was a bit melancholy, and it was very hot. As I turned my head to look in the other direction an unexpected cool breeze brushed over my entire body. I realized in that moment how much of life I took for granted. Before that evening I had given little importance to the perfect timing of a gentle breeze giving such relief. It was a small occurrence of joy, but I vowed to reverence others. I decided to be radically thankful for unexpected moments of pleasure and relief that I experienced.

Since that day, I have made written and mental lists of all that occur. Girls, that's making lemonade—no fairy tale wedding (not yet), but lots of things to celebrate and be thankful for daily. Take a look at just a few of what I call **radi-grats** listed below. (There I go again creating more of my own language.) I encourage you to begin observing those in your life. Just reviewing some of them makes me want to cry—with joy! **(+II)**

- ☆ Finding a $20.00 bill I forgot all about when payday is days away
- ☆ On an outing with my niece, she tugs at me and mistakenly calls me Momma

* Receiving a $1.00 off coupon on an item I really need
* Nothing on TV...finding a channel with a movie that turns out to be great
* Plans for the beach...it's overcast and the sun finally comes out
* Having a car picnic because it begins to rain
* Catching a key tennis match that I didn't realize was on TV
* The taste of ice water after a good work-out!
* Finding that I have some of my favorite dessert leftover in the fridge
* Finding out that I made my sales goal by $40.00
* A passing neighbor with 13 roses gives me one on the way to his sweetheart on Valentine's Day
* Realizing that I don't mind my moments alone
* Realizing I have the item at home that I forgot at the grocery store
* Discovering I can still "jam" (dance) like I use to
* Finding out that I get off work one hour earlier than I expected

Nothing but LEMONADE!

Girls, this radical stance of intentionally celebrating small unexpected occurrences has enhanced my entire life. This life tool enabled me to begin the process of re-imagining my journey as a single woman. I no longer judge the value of my life by what's not happening. Rather, I am constantly making note of that which enhances or edifies my existence as I am. You will be surprised at how many occur within the same day. Embracing this mindset increases the value of everyday living. Thus, it enables you to look hopefully toward the future and be less inclined to waste energy on the past. As a result, this life affirming approach could enable you to forgive others and even forgive yourself for past mistakes. Both of these are vital steps in successfully moving forward emotionally and psychologically.

You see, this single life, as it is, deserves to be celebrated! I know it's not easy—swl-lers—we are so hard on ourselves. But you must intentionally appreciate the fact that you were given life and strive to make the most of it. Now let's move on and review some other life tools that may help. Now, girls, did you enjoy that bit of lemonade? Told you we would get to it! **(+III)**

Christian Sidebars

(+I) The idea that God may have chosen me to remain single did not sit well with me. Growing up, as I stated earlier, I was immersed in literary romantic relationships and fantasy. I was one of the ones who longed for the Cinderella ending. As my faith grew and years passed I had to face the possibility that I might live out the purpose for my life single. I had to take comfort in Luke 12:31 which reminds us not to worry but to focus on God's kingdom and whatever we need will be provided for us. As Christian women we are admonished not to be conformed to the world (Romans 12:2, KJV) but to let God transform us into a new person and ultimately change the way we think. Of course, my prayer has always been that my desire and God's plan for me would quickly cross paths.

(+III) It is a challenge to be thankful for everything (1 Thess. 5:18). My strategy to elevate the importance of simple everyday life occurrences stems from this Christian principle. Life can be fulfilling if we intentionally think on things that are true, honorable, right, pure, lovely, and admirable (Phil. 4:8). I realized that my decision to creatively counteract the negative thoughts and feelings that can plague single life reflected my growth as a Christian.

(+III) As I stated earlier, the scripture that dictates my way of life is John 10:10, "I am come that they might have life, and that they might have it more abundantly." (KJV) Once I decided that I would proactively appreciate life and all of its blessings the anxiety of living single became manageable. Let me be clear, it didn't dissipate; it just didn't overwhelm me as much!

Chapter Seven

The Misplaced Lives of Eve

So you think life is over since you can't find the man of your dreams and get married? For years, I fell prostrate literally, crying out why not me? Then I discovered something, after revisiting a list of life goals I had created as a much younger woman. I am so much more than a forgotten prospect for marital bliss! There in front of me were the lives I refused to pursue fully because I decided nothing was more important than getting married.

I say lives, because I believe that each passion or interest we pursue requires its own energy and produces its own network or circle of relationships and social interactions. I took inventory, checking off those things that I had accomplished. The results were not good. What had happened to my desire to become financially independent, to travel abroad, to learn a new language, to getting into the best shape of my life, to learning to salsa, or my passion for starting my own business, becoming a better writer, advocating for the poor and plus size demographics, or winning a trophy for playing tennis on any level?

In essence, I had forgotten who I really was in my chase to the altar. I had forgotten the little girl growing up in the housing projects promising to cultivate all my interests. I wanted to be one of the most well-read, well-travelled, cultured, and accomplished broads on the planet. How could I have allowed my search for a spouse to interrupt this goal to be so alive and present? What a detour! **(+I)** I spent my early years as an adult (on and off), depressed, unfulfilled, overweight, and self-defeated.

Well, there were extenuating circumstances. Sure, I grew up during a time when women were told to find their husbands in college—sure, all of my family members and most of my peers got married at least once—but what if I had fought convention and fully focused my time and energy toward my true self?

Girls, I'd probably be soaking up the sun on the French Riviera or sailing around the Greek Isles right now! Yeah, I know what Billy Dee Williams said to Diana Ross in the movie *Mahogany*, "Success is nothing without someone to share it with."* Much wiser now, I know that Diana should have retorted that as great a travesty is regret and unfulfilled potential.

Once, during a speech at a college assembly, I heard the greatest endorsement for self-fulfillment: "The universe actually shrinks when someone does not fulfill their destiny."* So how can I keep you from making my mistake? Keep you from wasting a lot of time, energy, and opportunity? Keep you, like me, from refusing to become who you are…more so…refusing to insist on becoming who you are, like (Ralph Waldo) Emerson stated?* What advice can I give you for pursuing life fully…for re-imagining your life right where you are? So who are you, really?

Oftentimes we forget as we age and try to make sense of our experiences. Unavoidably our lives are shaped or misshaped by so many outside influences. Do you remember what you dreamed of becoming? More important, do you remember when you first began to allow the desires of your peers or family members to become your desires?

It starts much earlier than we realize. The example of the youngest girl amongst three sisters in Chapter Three is well worth mentioning here again. You see, you could tell that she really wanted to become a fashion model. She made it clear every time she posed for pictures or when she entered a room demanding the spotlight. As she grew older, I waited to see if she would pursue her dream—I hoped she would at least try. She succumbed to the pressure—she's in her mid-twenties now and she's having babies like her sisters. That's not a travesty—but I bet the universe shrank a bit at her decision. **(+II)**

You know, fear, like societal/family expectations, can be a deterrent as well in our quest to be true to ourselves. During my last year of undergraduate study, we travelled to New York City, one of the fashion capitals of the world. I had known since I was a young girl, that I wanted a fashion career. I wanted to be a designer or make some significant contribution to the fashion industry. While there, I felt an incredible pull to remain in the city—like it was where I belonged! But I grew up somewhat sheltered, and no one in my family had ever taken such a bold step as moving so far away at such a young age.

This was many years ago—and not many others in my class heeded the advice of our professors who urged us to "go to the fashion centers of the world if you want to be successful." So because I was afraid, I went back home after I completed my degree in Clothing/Textiles & Fashion Merchandising. (And the universe shrank a bit). I went home unfulfilled and started a career with a local retailer and began attending the many weddings and showers that become a part of a 20-something's life. There was no possible way that I wouldn't become consumed with the idea of getting married.

Then again, I often wonder now if I never chose to marry because it just wasn't enough for me. Oops! Can I say that? I couldn't in the 80s. Folk would have thought something was wrong with me. Of course, some of you, even after reading this chapter, will concentrate fully on nothing else. "Getting your man" is your theme song. You will refuse to believe you will end up like me. I never thought it possible either. And who am I to judge?

It took me many years to realize that I had neglected to focus on the other meaningful areas of my life. But listen, I am serious about this, girls, because I have been where you are and if you remain single many years, I know what you will face in the future. I must insist that you cultivate other interests and discover other things that you care deeply about. It will enrich your life and increase your chances of meeting new people. Trust me, as the years go by, it will be a refreshing relief to know that the possibility of finding Mr. Right literally exists. So I say it again, broaden your horizons and embrace your other "lives." But don't get it twisted, girls, I am still peeping…the desire to have one last great love affair is as much a part of my life as ever!

But until your desire becomes a reality…turn yourself on…I knew y'all would go there…I'm not talking about that! That's a discussion in another chapter.

I'm not kidding…seriously…do you think you are interesting? Would you date or more pertinent marry yourself? It is said that we attract what we give off. What vibes or signals do you project? Are you sending desperate, forlorn messages when you encounter the world? **Are you enjoying single life**?

Or do you ritually review your wedding plans over and over again…like I did…LOL even when there isn't even an actual prospect? Do you turn down opportunities to see the world because he is just not the one? Are all your friends and acquaintances in the same circle—have the same interests? Is there something you have been dying to experience, a place you want to visit, something new you want to learn or some drastic change you want to make?

Maybe you have been pouring too much energy into finding a mate because you can't find the courage to do that something! Heaven forbid, like I did…are you desperately waiting around for that same guy who clearly is not going to marry you? Don't be like me and learn later (almost too late), that your time is precious and valuable. Embrace the fact now!! **(+III)** You see, now, at 50-something, I am trying to do all the stuff I should have focused on earlier; things I am just as passionate about.

Speaking of passion—it's what I vow to live with even if I am single until death! It is said that humans only use a small portion of their brains, but I think a greater deficit is the amount of passion we get to expend in our everyday lives. I once expressed to one of my married girlfriends that I wanted passion in my relationship with a man. She asked me to explain what I meant. At the time, she had been married fifteen or more years. Girls, seems that marriage and passion are oxymoronic. Is it possible that what I was looking for and what some of you are looking for must come from within, drawn out by some other stimuli, other than another individual?

Not long ago, I started my dress-making business. I planned to launch my first line of dresses in a spring fashion show. Unbelievably, the two days before the fashion show, I had only two hours of sleep. I was so exhilarated by the work that I never got tired during the entire three days of the event. From this experience, I learned a critical life lesson. It is up to me to generate passion in my life. So I declare now and forever to work, play, and serve with passion!

It is obvious from the illustration above that passion produces energy and increases productivity. If you are not involved in those things that you love to do you are constantly depleting your energy and not living life to its fullest.

Many of us hate our daily jobs. Even so, I decided to perform my job at the highest possible level and then reward myself by playing even harder at the things I love to do. As well, I decided to continue to pursue other fulfilling opportunities that could move me toward financial independence, like my dress business. To balance things, after hard work and intentional play and relaxation, I would find causes that I care deeply about and serve others.

Now, girls, raise your right hand and repeat after me, "No matter what, I vow to pursue passion in work, play and serving others!" (Whenever possible.) With this schedule, Mr. Right will have to make an appointment to see us. Yeah baby, no doubt, we're enjoying some lemonade now! **(+IV)**

Christian Sidebars

(**+I**) Oftentimes we try to tell God what should be happening in our lives. Instead of communing with God (individually and corporately) to discover our destinies and life purpose, we make choices using our own wisdom. There's an old saying that God laughs when we make plans! Jeremiah 29:11 makes clear whose wisdom we should rely upon: "For surely I know the plans I have for you, says the Lord, plans for your good and not for disaster, to give you a future with hope." As my faith grew I realized that the one who created me would know what was best for me. TD Jakes, the renowned television evangelist stated that if someone walks out of your life, let them go; they are just not a part of God's ultimate plan for you. Move on! I know…sometimes that's easier said than done.

(**+II**) The sooner you believe in God's unique plan for your life the less likely you will be influenced by the lives of those around you. Unfortunately, we spend a lot of time when we are younger trying to conform to others. Hosea 6:3a reminds us of what we should do instead if we want to have a peaceful existence in our own skins, Oh, that we might know the Lord. Let us press on to know him! In our effort to know God, we find ourselves and our life purpose.

(**+III**) We think that we have all the time in the world. I certainly did. Before I knew it, I was fifty-something and more than half of my life goals were incomplete. I had spent so much time trying to become like others around me. Proverbs 12:11b insists that only fools idle away their time or senselessly chase fantasies. This bit of wisdom may seem harsh, but it takes a lot of courage and steadfastness to follow your own path. As well, it ain't easy to overcome the fear and stress that can accompany being alone. Single women who decide to embrace life fully can be empowered by these words from God to Joshua, who led the Israelites after Moses' death: I hear by command you: Be strong and courageous; do not be frightened or dismayed, for the Lord your God is with you wherever you go (1:9).

(+IV) I know that my passion for life stems from my faith in Christ. Jesus summons me to live fully as evidenced in John 10:10. He came, died, and rose from the grave so that I may have a rich and satisfying life. I made this promise a personal mandate after realizing how much I took for granted and how much life offered despite being single.

Chapter Eight

A Table for One, Please!

One afternoon, one of my closest married girlfriends at the time called me in excitement. She exclaimed, "I finally did it!"

She was calling me from a local restaurant and had gotten up the nerve to dine alone. For a long time, she had wondered how I was able to accomplish this social feat over and over again. I wanted to share her excitement, but for her it was just some random excursion, since most of the time she and her husband or friends (like me) dined out together. For me, it was a way of life. And, girls, if you remain single long enough and want to honor your single lifestyle, it won't be a problem for you either!

What do I mean by honor your lifestyle? I pause now, because I want to be sure you hear me.

You do not need anyone's permission to live your life!

You were given that privilege the moment you took your first breath. If other folk really had that power, you would be surprised at the persons who would gladly snuff the life out of you. (Have you watched any of *The Purge* movies?) Forget them!!

I order you, right now, to grasp life and go anywhere you want to go, confidently and alone (wisely—as street savvy as possible). You'd be amazed at how creative you will get at accommodating yourself. This country is a source of so many contradictions. It promotes individualism and self-sufficiency on one hand (obviously for men) and on the other it makes us ashamed of being alone (messages from mass media and society). **(+I)** Frankly, it's just more propaganda that women must endure.

Girls, I love the comedian/actor Chris Tucker…you hear me…I love Chris Tucker; if polygamy was legal in the U.S. I would even be his second wife. (Yeah, I said it, all of us got at least one man we would be number two for, LOL).

Not too long ago he was in town doing stand-up. I didn't care how much it was gonna cost or if anyone else I knew wanted to see him. Sure, it would have been great to have a date or drag along a friend, but in the end, I got to share my love for my favorite comedian on my own.

Now I understand that everyone won't be able to instantly attend social events or activities alone. (At 50-something, I still get self-conscious at times). But I see it as a form of disrespect to keep denying ourselves the fruits of life.

So you're single…can't always get a date, friends forsake you as well, make lemonade girl! Make lemonade! Try it, and if it feels uncomfortable, keep trying it, and before long the confidence it builds will spill over into other areas of your life.

There's no doubt that movies imitate real life dilemmas and situations, but often they too can provide us with new perspectives for living. One useful example for this chapter is the advice Harry Connick Jr. gives to the newly single Sandra Bullock (Birdee) in the movie *Hope Floats.** They both are dining alone in a local restaurant when Connick Jr. (Justin) gets up from his table to leave and he pauses to say, "It's not for sissies (dining alone). The trick is to seem mysterious…like it's your choice."

And wouldn't it be phenomenal if we swl-lers lived as if being single was our choice? You see, girls, this is one of the purposes for my book. I wanted to promote a new way of thinking about living single and I hoped to infuse a vibrant narrative into a supposed disenchanting lifestyle. Over the years, I have been challenged socially by my single status, but I have also been determined to appreciate and enjoy life fully. So I want to present to you some of the ways I uniquely dealt with time alone or socially being on my own.

Remember the lemonism "Always have **Plan B** when single and dating"? This advice was given to me by a male friend after I was disappointed by an anticipated date that fell through. He simply cautioned me to be prepared to enjoy myself socially regardless of setbacks or things occurring that I could not control. The wonderful thing that began to happen over the years as I developed what I call **"personal rituals"** (another life tool) is that these practices utilized as Plan B took on **Plan A** status.

Let me explain. For this book's purposes, Plan A activities or events are the preferred societal practice for any social activity or major holiday:

Women are expected to attend restaurants, movies, concerts, parties, and other social events accompanied by someone. Your boss invites you to a dinner party; there should be no problem getting your boyfriend/spouse or **BFF** to accompany you.

You should have the most interesting details on Monday to report at the "water cooler" about the fabulous time you and "Paul, Dick, or Harry" had over the weekend.

Your birthday should be this grand celebratory event made complete with the man in your life by your side.

It's February 14 and you are expected to get two dozen yellow roses to outshine the dozen red ones all your co-workers will receive at work.

It's vacation season again and you should be deciding where you and "Joe" will be going this year (or whether you can bear being away from him for a separate vacation with the girls).

It's November and the holidays are approaching, and you should be wondering how you and "Joe" are going to get to see both your families. (Or will you finally get that proposal and diamond ring?)

And it's the week of New Year's Eve and "Joe" should be surprising you with a trip to watch the ball drop in New York City, or taking you to some other glitzy affair where you get to kiss passionately at midnight.

Girls, I know...you want me to stop the torture and get to the lemonade for this chapter. Alright, I think I've made my point. **(+II)**

Now, I know that some of you are thinking that I am taking family and good friends for granted. But over the years, I have told both groups face-to-face, that spending time with them and tagging along with them everywhere gets old!

If you remain single for many years, you gotta have Plan B. And when you begin to truly honor your single life Plan B practices will become as important to your existence as any other. In fact, you may find yourself longing for a Plan B activity while experiencing one of the supposed ideal scenarios of Plan A. Most of my "personal rituals," as no doubt will yours, center around things I love to do. The key is to give them credence by naming them and scheduling them to correspond with traditional social events and activities. Check out my list, girls!

"No Foreplay" Weekends

This is my formula for having great weekends! If you have no significant other or no official date for the weekend, starting Thursday, make an effort to stay away from **all** romantic music (no Luther Vandross or KEM for me), TV shows, commercials (if you can), and movies (watch only action flicks), etc. because they can subliminally provoke emotional meltdowns. (As well, avoid all ex-entanglements, LOL.) But do intentionally play, relax, and serve others doing the things you love as mentioned earlier. And for extra assurance, try to tweeze in a physical fitness activity between Friday evening and Saturday morning. **(+III)** More on that subject in the next chapter.

Weekly V-Day

I love live cut flowers. I have enjoyed my share of red roses from suitors. Of course, that changed a bit over the years. So I started buying myself cut flowers weekly for my dining room table. If I get an extra dozen on Valentine's Day, it's gravy! Or just one, like I mentioned on my list of radi-grats—nothing pleases me more.

"All the Things I Love" Birthday Celebration

This has become my favorite "personal ritual." It often can take two days to complete. I celebrate my birthday by enjoying all my favorite things. Activities usually include a scented bubble bath by candlelight with my favorite adult beverage and my favorite music piped into the bathroom. Before or after, I have my favorite dinner and dessert and watch my favorite movie. For gifts, I shop my favorite clothing store, or buy my favorite fragrance or purchase new music by my favorite artist. You get the picture!

Vacations at Wimbledon

I am lucky that I am such an avid tennis fan. I am hesitant to be anywhere that keeps me from watching the game at the height of its season (May-August). I have even taken vacation time off from work just to watch some of the more important tournaments like Wimbledon and the U.S. Open. I am as passionate about tennis as I have been at finding Mr. Right. In fact, I could care less about finding him when I am watching a great tennis match! Oops, in this case, love does equal 0 for me. Hopefully, one day soon I can travel to see these tournaments and watch them live!

Breakfast/Dinner and a Movie

My favorite meal is breakfast. I can eat breakfast foods anytime of the day. And I don't have to tell you how much I love watching movies. The two activities paired together is a bit of heaven! This is my go-to plan if I find that I will be spending Thanksgiving or Christmas alone. Yes, it happens. It doesn't occur often, but sometimes I can't get home to share with my family. I shouldn't encourage you, but try actually going to a 10 a.m. movie at the theatre and sneaking in a full-course breakfast meal. Naughty...I know...but what fun!!

New Year's on the Shell

I owe my ability to create rituals from my mother! She was never financially well off, but she enriched our lives with what she had. As a family we spent the New Year shucking steamed oysters and toasting one another once the ball dropped on TV. If I don't have a date or if I can't get to my family, I make sure I have oysters to steam (I lasted the longest at the table) and once the ball drops, I call all my immediate family members to wish them Happy New Year! The time it takes to do this can keep you from being sad that there's no one there to kiss into the New Year. **(+IV)**

Again, as the years pass, you will be surprised at how much reverence you will give to your Plan B activities. Of course, I hope that all of you will find Mr. Right and not suffer socially the number of years that I did. (Even though, that's not a given). Just in case, remember, it's your choice. You can choose to honor your single lifestyle by going anywhere socially you want and by creating your own "personal rituals" to enrich your time alone or you can be a "sissy" like Harry Connick, Jr. implied (no offense to anyone), afraid to embrace life fully and worried constantly about what other folk think. Girls, make me proud, which is making lemonade?

Christian Sidebars

(+I) Even though God promises in Hebrews 13:5-6 that he will never leave or forsake us, I must admit that even now, after many years, the stigma of being alone can still sting. But I have also been restored by some of the most beautiful prose found in scripture, Romans 8:35-39. Verses 38-39 make clear the depth of God's love for us: "I am convinced, the Apostle Paul writes from Corinth, that neither death, nor life, nor angels, nor rulers, nor things present, nor things to come, nor powers, nor height, nor depth, nor anything else in all creation will be able to separate us from the love of God in Christ Jesus our Lord." (KJV)

(+II) Even with great faith, it is hard to exist amongst our peers and not long for the experiences of romance, love, and marriage that we observe. However, as we mature in our faith we understand that God is pleased most when we focus our energies on those things not of the world. The second chapter of I John explains: "Do not love the world or the things in the world. The Love of the Father is not in those who love the world; for all that is in the world—the desire of the flesh, the desire of the eyes, the pride of riches—comes not from the Father but the world. And the world and its desires are passing away, but those who do the will of God live forever." (15-16, KJV)

(+III) Though we're living in the 21st century, women still struggle for autonomy. Women on the whole feel more comfortable and worthy when they are in relationships and when they are interacting socially accompanied by someone. But should a single woman stop experiencing life just because she may be alone? The Apostle Paul advises us in his letter to the Philippians (4:11-13, KJV) that one of the secrets to life is learning to be content no matter where we find ourselves. It is crucial that single women learn to be satisfied with their lives and be confident that God has plans for them to prosper.

(+IV) Many churches have created New Year's Eve services to attend. The African Americans' Watch Night is a tradition that has lasted since the ending of slavery. Starting the New Year uplifting God can be a blessing and an opportunity for spiritual renewal. Besides, it is always a good idea for us to worship amongst fellow Christians—no matter the season!

Chapter Nine

Orgasm, a Girl's Best Friend

Caught ya! Girls, did you skip over to this chapter of the book just to read about the elusive orgasm? 'Might as well come clean, this chapter is not going to cover what you think! At least not to the extent you imagined. I have been pretty transparent throughout this conversation and this is definitely not the time to shut down. This topic is vital to our discussion!

You know that whenever you find a health checklist, the question arises. I have not seen one yet where the subject is not addressed: Do you have a healthy sex life? How often do you have sex?

Usually if you answer, "multiple times a week," it increases your health score. So our engagement in sexual activity is vital to our health. Girls, I know y'all are glad to hear that!

Oh, don't get prudish now. (Or get outta hand looking for partners.) The fact that sexual activity contributes to overall health should relieve some of your guilt about it. I know how difficult the subject is for many people to discuss, but it is life, pure and simple. I had a male friend put it just that way...and he was right, even though he had an ulterior motive when he said it! **(+I)**

Speaking of ulterior motives—author Denene Millner offers some insightful suggestions in her 1997 book, *The Sistahs' Rules*, to determine if the man in your life is just seeing you for the "nookie."* Read Rule # Twenty if you dare to know the truth about your relationship.

And just in case you are one of those swl-lers who struggles with your own sexuality, I suggest again that you read *Sex and the Single Girl* by Helen Gurley Brown. She knocks it out of the park in Chapter Four, detailing how to be sexy. In timeless fashion, she empowers women to embrace their femininity and sensuality.*

Now the subject of orgasms is another matter altogether. The title of the chapter is a bit misleading since many (quite a few) women actually struggle to achieve this level of sexual excitement.

So, girls, I have to drop a bombshell, that is, if you think that getting a husband will ensure that you have quality sexual experiences. Let's keep it real! Sex and love can be two different things. That's why Dr. Ruth, a sex therapist, and doctors specializing in ED and impotence have jobs. There are women completely dissatisfied sexually with their spouses. I could name names or cite examples, but this is too sensitive of a topic. I surely would lose married friends.

Now, one source had this to say: "Orgasms are a mystery to many people, even to those who have them."[*] According to an article found in the June 2018 issue of *Woman's Day* online, as many as one in three women have trouble reaching orgasms when having sex.[*]

Girls, that's one-third of us. But get this—as many as 80 percent of women have difficulty experiencing orgasms during intercourse. I guess we aren't so friendly with the orgasm cuz it gets worse—43 percent of women suffer from FSD, (Female Sexual Dysfunction), the inability to experience an orgasm at all.[*]

Heyyyyy, I can sense some of you thinking, "Why bother if you can't experience the ultimate gratification?" Sexual therapist Dr. Ruth disagrees in her recent book, *The Doctor Is In, Dr. Ruth on Love, Life and Joie de Vivre,* since she advises a woman to stop concentrating on achieving orgasm and just enjoy every aspect of the love-making process.[*] See, girls, this is probably not the worst idea, since it could eventually lead to the ecstatic moment. The French think it's enough to die for since they describe the feelings after experiencing an orgasm as *la petite mort*, "the little death," referring to the total depletion of energy that occurs.[*]

Girls, I know you're asking where the heck this discussion is going since it's obvious that I will not be providing tips on how to achieve an orgasm, LOL! You might want to check out other books by Dr. Ruth K. Westheimer with Pierre A. Lehu and other experts for further assistance in that area. But this chapter will focus most on another byproduct of sexual activity. Thankfully, it can be produced by other means since single women can find themselves inactive sexually for periods of time. **(+II)**

No, y'all, I am not gonna talk about the toys and other paraphernalia. So what you talkin 'bout, I hear you ask? **Endorphins,** honey! Those natural opiates found in the brain that are known to relieve stress, enhance pleasure, and lead to feelings of happiness, even to euphoria.

Guess what? There are other physical activities that release these hormones. Look, our overall physical health and mindset is crucial to maintaining a well-balanced life. So when you're honoring your single life by being on your own and not compromising your standards, girls, make sure you're routinely exercising, dancing your nights away, and adding all the laughter to your life that you can stand!

Think it doesn't work? Like I stated before, it's been documented that endorphins are released during sexual activity. But I figured it out long before I had it confirmed by my research. I put two and two together. I observed how great I felt after a good work-out, after dancing to my favorite music all night, and after laughing so hard my chest hurt. And no, it doesn't completely replace it, I'm not gonna lie! But it comes really close, and it is making lemonade out of the situation!

Yeah, they are right, girls. "Milk does a body good," but you could easily replace the beverage in this famous ad with exercise. I cannot say enough about how important exercise is to physical and emotional stability. In fact, I will go as far to say that, "you must exercise for sanity." Remember those endorphins!!

You see, if you are not involved in some type of physical fitness activity, you're not fighting depression, also known as the blues—that tell you things are hopeless—are never gonna change. I am not the fittest person in the world, but I have engaged in some type of physical activity on and off since I was a very young adult. I started walking, highly recommended by medical professionals, and later I enjoyed playing tennis, roller skating, bike riding, and participating in low-impact aerobics classes.

As I have gotten older I have added strength training (weights) to my workout routine since my metabolism has taken an expected hit from aging. So if your strategy for maintaining health and well-being does not include exercise you're making a gigantic mistake. Yes, I said gigantic! **(+III)**

Remember our pledge to work, play, and serve with passion. Exercise has to find its way into that schedule. (See, now there is even less time to stress over finding Mr. Right). The therapeutic benefits of just a 30-minute workout 3 times a week are incredible. (Of course you should get your doctor to approve it before you start.)

I can have the most stressful day, or I can be feeling frustrated from the ills of being single, or I can be irritable because I have let days pass without my usual work out and presto, after 30 minutes of vigorous exercise I feel brand new. In fact, I am better than that; I am confident, renewed, and ready to take on the world. And talk about a good night's rest. I tell you, girls, if you have trouble sleeping, maintain a regular schedule of physical fitness activities and you will sleep like a baby. Believe me, the positive effects of exercise are just too good to be true! I know; someone should pay me to promote it. If you want a medical endorsement go to the website of the Mayo Clinic, one of the best hospitals in the country, and read their article on the seven benefits of regular physical activity. I tell you, the rewards are priceless!

After I left home, I found out that I had something else in common with my mother when she shared that she always made sure she watched her favorite television sitcoms before she went to bed at night. She knew that a good laugh before laying down for the night was beneficial. Of course, she was able to do this because television stations began running marathon episodes of syndicated shows. No, I don't think she knew about the endorphins, but she was a wise old soul!

Maya Angelou, renowned poet and author, was once asked what the secret for successful living was and she answered, "You must make sure you laugh as much as you cry."* Girls, you can't live a more balanced life than that. And yes, laughing is physical activity since the diaphragm is muscular tissue which aids the release of the cackling sounds. I am not a doctor, but I know that there is quite a release of tension from my entire body when the sounds reverberate from my vocal cords. After completing my research, I wondered if the endorphins released from one individual's laughter could somehow influence the mood of another. Maybe that's why they say that laughter can be contagious.

I remember having lunch with one of my good girlfriends at the mall and as usual we cracked our sides laughing and carrying on. One other customer in the restaurant, dining alone, got up to leave and stopped at our table. She actually thanked us for making her feel better. That's a powerful testimony for adding as much laughter to your life as possible. **(+IV)** Of course, mind your manners— that could have easily been an admonishment to keep the noise down!

Now I know everyone is not a great dancer. At least not the free-style mode I enjoy. I do what I call "silhouette dancing." I place a spotlight against a wall in a dark room and watch my rhythmic movements cast shadows. It's great fun if you are on your own. But if you need company try one of the line dances created by R&B, Country, or Hip-Hop music. Or simply take ballroom or Latin dance classes. Dancing can be fun and exciting for everyone. Of course, it has always been something I love to do.

Don't say it! What don't I love? Sorry, remember how much I wanted to be an all-around cultured prodigy? Don't hate, I just got rhythm! But there are so many other activities that you could engage in that promote physical fitness. Find one, two if your schedule will allow. (And that's two outside of structured workout routines.) The key is to get those endorphins flowing regularly so that you can offset the frustration and craziness of single life—of life period! **(+V)**

I know you don't believe that these things will offset the lack of a healthy sex life. For most of you, especially those of you not yet thirty, celibacy is not going to be an option. Heck, I know you over-sexed 40 and 50-something-year-olds are looking at me like I'm crazy! (Well, at the page). LOL.

I hear you thinking, "She can't believe that we are gonna save ourselves until we're married." Dr. Ruth, in the book mentioned earlier, reminds us that there is no such thing as safe sex, "less risky sex" is more accurate, since condoms can break and not function properly.[*] Unfortunately, being chaste is the only way to completely guard against all STDs (and unwanted pregnancies).

No way, I hear you reply! But let's be serious; remember earlier I mentioned that our African-American sisters are suffering with HIV/AIDS in large numbers. Your life is precious, and you deserve to meet Mr. Right and live happily ever after. I know this single walk, to quote Langston Hughes, "ain't been no crystal stair," but the choices you make can sour the journey or sweeten it like lemonade.[*] Please be responsible and treasure your life and future!

Christian Sidebars

(+I) Society today is so secularized that premarital sex is a foregone conclusion. Nevertheless, the Bible makes it clear for believers that sexual activity should occur within the confines of marriage (Proverbs 5:18-19; Hebrews 13:4; I Corinthians 6:18). So, regardless of what we think, it is a significant tenant of our faith. There are other perspectives, but in the end as single Christians we have to struggle with this expectation. I tried challenging the tenant early on as a Christian and I experienced so much disappointment and regret that I soon realized that excluding this type of intimacy can be revelatory in choosing genuine partners. Simply put, God knows best!

(+II) I know…some of us…a lot of us commit to our faith when we are far from being physical virgins. It's unfortunate because going cold turkey is what Dr. Tony Evans insists that we must do once we are enlightened—the old life is gone and a new life begins (II Corinthians 5:17). Scripture verses I Corinthians 6:19-20 convict us further by reminding us that our bodies are not our own and that they house the Holy Spirit. We single girls would be in big trouble if not for God's grace, forgiveness and understanding. Thankfully, sanctification is a lifetime process.

(+III) In the opening to John's third letter he emphasizes both the physical health and soul of his reader. "I hope all is well with you and that you are as healthy in body as you are strong in spirit." (1:2) This equal treatment of the two matters support my belief that a healthy body is crucial to maintaining a fulfilling life. Of course, this is an opportune time to interject that you can't have good health without some type of physical fitness activity. You just can't!!

(+IV) Proverbs 17:22a states, "A cheerful heart is good medicine." Enuff said!

(+V) Even King David danced and leaped in celebration when he and the Israelites brought the ark into Jerusalem (II Samuel 6: 14, 16). Like David, we too can express our joy frivolously through dance as we thank God for the blessing of physical and mental health and for simply being alive!

Chapter Ten

Beauty Does Matter!

Remember those groom-free days I talked about in Chapter One? Those can't go on forever! Much as I love those days, girls, I must find the energy to pull myself together and present the most fabulous me possible. Of course, fabulous is in the eye of the beholder. People casually make the statement that "beauty is just skin deep" so that they will not appear superficial. But let's not delude ourselves about the importance of physical appearance for women in America and let's be honest in most of the world. (+I)

Unashamed, I have boldly stated in the title for this chapter what few of us are willing to admit. I have no qualms about stressing how important it is for us to optimize our external appearance. And not just because men are visual creatures—even though it is true. In the September 2014 edition of *Essence*, hot new blogger, 27-year-old Cipriana Quann had this to say: "Beauty means healthy hair, skin, teeth, and nails. All of these components can make a style."[*]

This is an interesting unconventional way to define beauty and it is an achievement we all can reach in our goal to be fabulous. Girls, you know our doctors and dentists will be glad to assist us in adopting this standard. Of course, there are some other practices for beauty and "glam" that are a part of my personal regimen that I share with you later. In closing out the chapter, I discuss why maximizing our fabulousness is so important in our quest for quality life.

Wanna know how I measure my effort toward maintaining my fabulous self? I know you gonna think it sounds "old school." Girls, can you remember or are you experiencing the feelings generated from a new man in your life or the possibility of love? Both provide the most incredible zap of energy and the most heightened awareness of oneself imaginable. I don't have to tell y'all, do I? At least I hope that you've all had a taste of it at least once in your life. (If I could bottle the feeling, I would become a billionaire.) During my last romance, I just wanted to dance. I would put on my favorite music and his favorite outfit, and I would fantasize the evening away. (He was a long-distance boo.) I know, don't rub it in, right? But when I am in this euphoric state I conduct the most comprehensive grooming workout possible. Power Grooming! Girls, I groom and beautify every inch of my being from the top of my head to the heels of my crusty feet. Don't laugh. That long-distance relationship didn't last; but what a gift of life and what memories it created to call upon. (Girls, did you see how I turned that into more lemonade?)

So when I am not in a euphoric state, I can take inventory of how well I am taking care of myself using the standard above. Even now as I write this, I notice unmanicured nails, my dry un-soaked feet, and the lack of luxurious fragrances from my hair and body. You guessed it! There ain't a man in sight. I can hear the feminists say what a turnabout I have made since the chapter about groom-free days. Hey, I will be the first to admit that I have some ambiguity about my single life. Look, I cut my teeth on the fantasy of finding a great love, even though I am a master at making lemonade. A lot of you share my mixed feelings according to the September 2015 issue of *Elle*. According to a survey in the magazine of thirty-something swl-lers, 57% say they would be happy to remain single and yet half of them wish they were in relationships and most of them (75%) can't even find someone they are interested in dating.[*]

But the truth is the truth even if it doesn't support a particular agenda. Women are greatly influenced by the men in their lives. Of course, I know too that we deserve to treat ourselves well, romantic interest or not. It happens though; we sometimes lack motivation and get lazy about caring for ourselves over time. If you find that you are "in this funk" you need to take stock and give yourself a tune-up and become that fabulous person you are. It's never too late to begin again. Can I repeat that? It's never too late to begin again!

I know y'all are itching to know what my Power Grooming routine includes. Whenever I am in a euphoric state, I rarely have dates on Friday evenings. Got to get the grooming in! But my routine could include any of the following, if you touch up mid-week some of it won't need repeating. My workout actually starts with my forehead, since I don't do anything for my hair. I have professionals for care, chemicals, and cuts. Now here's how I get FABULOUS! Once I have wrapped my hair up securely I get started.

First, I make sure I have a weekly mud facial that exfoliates and brightens the skin, giving it vibrancy. There are tons of products on the market to choose from.

Before the facial, I remove all unwanted hair, now that I am 50-something that would include hair from my upper lip. **LMHO**.

My eyebrows would have already been shaped by a local professional since this procedure can be performed quite inexpensively. My own eyelashes are long, but fake eyelashes and professionally applied lashes are the rave. On some occasions I opt for the fake lashes for drama and sex appeal.

I love candlelight aromatherapy bubble baths (with music). And so, if I have had a very stressful week I look forward to this indulgence accompanied by my favorite glass of wine (oops, or lemonade cocktail) making this deluxe pampering.

Before my luxurious bath I make sure my legs, bikini and underarm areas have been shaved; the soothing bath also becomes a pre-soak for my finger and toe nail care. (Of course, some cultures don't find hair on the body unappealing).

Once I have dragged myself from the bath, I moisturize my entire body right away with my favorite scented lotions and creams.

As well, I go through the 3 steps, cleanse, tone, and moisturize for my face, of course by this time, hopefully I have removed the mud mask. LOL.

Finally, I prepare to complete both a manicure and pedicure. Yes, I still give myself both despite the trend to go to nail shops. This process can take a bit of time since you have to wait for both set of nails to dry.

Finally, I let my hair down, put on my favorite fragrance and lightly apply some make-up. If I am in a euphoric state, I may change my mind about that Friday night date and test the effects of my effort. If not, I get to feel completely made over, not to mention FABULOUS!

One additional thought: Do keep abreast of new beauty and fashion trends. Maintaining an updated look all-around goes a long way in keeping an upbeat and positive outlook. Of course, implement those things that enhance your style and appeal.

I intentionally made the decision to cover the issue of beauty and external appeal in the last chapter of my book; (I guess I too didn't want to seem overly superficial) even though I believe that our external appearance can be as vital to the process of re-imagination as the intrinsic factors already discussed. Our romantic relationships as noted in Part I, are so fundamentally tied to our self-image and our self-worth. In order to successfully navigate our single lives—without these relationships—we need to remain as self-assured and well-balanced as possible. Though most people as I stated earlier will rhetorically claim that "beauty is just skin deep," I wisely choose to face the fact that the single woman needs an extra dose of confidence as she attempts to overcome the internal and external challenges that confront her. Confidence is built by all aspects of a person, including the enhancement of external appeal. It affirms us in a way that very little else does, except maybe love. So get to creating a lifetime beauty and grooming regimen of your own; one that makes you feel fabulous and even euphoric!

Christian Sidebars

(+I) Of course, I know well as Christians that we are asked to examine our hearts and not give importance to our outer appearance (I Peter 3:3, 5). Proverbs 31:30 expands this belief, "Charm is deceptive, and beauty does not last, but a woman who fears the Lord will be greatly praised." As Christians, our first concern should be who we are becoming spiritually, but just as Jesus was divine and human; we too must wrestle with our physical bodies and outer appeal. I believe that it is crucial to embrace and enhance both if we are to live full lives as single women in American society.

Chapter Eleven

The Acid Analysis

After realizing that our discussion would soon come to an end, I decided to look at other current sources addressing this issue of living single. Girls, there are tons of books, articles, and studies available! That's a slight exaggeration, but it affirmed my decision to add my perspective to a narrative that neglects to address the real needs and concerns of single women but utilizes clichés and rhetoric to tiptoe around the truth.

Of course, I am a veteran and I know that even after listening to the advice of others, single women still have to "walk the walk." So it is important that we first have our challenges and grief validated before we hear how easy it is to overcome them. It's not! I suffered through some awful, frustrating days from my late twenties through my early forties. It was a hellish period. Desperation...clock tickin'...time running out.

At twenty-four, the man I would end up loving most of my adult life got married to someone else! Nothing will make you less hopeful than that. Since I have always been a ferocious reader, guess what? I began reading self-help/inspirational books. I tried to find out what was wrong with me, what was wrong with him, why he chose someone other than me and I even sought strategies for getting him back. I know; a sure sign that I was out of it. Just thinking about it brings back the anguish of those days—the failure and the feelings of worthlessness and lost. Of course, I know now that this period of discovery was one of the defining moments of my personal life.

So before you dive into a similar undertaking for salvation, I want to give you the heads-up on three recent best-selling books that catapulted into pop culture infamy. Now, most of the books I read were just fluff—meaning that they did little to provide any real answers to questions I had about my specific circumstances. In fact, the hyperbole offered simply added to my stress, LOL, since it posed other questions about my personality and caused me to over-analyze myself. Hopefully the following brief reviews will help save some time, energy, and grief as you search for other resources as counsel. But y'all need to keep in mind that I am taking a stab at these writers as comeuppance since they nor their cohorts delivered me from a life as a swl-ler.

Grief or relief? That is the question I sought to answer for you in my examination of *The Rules II* (1997) by Ellen Fein and Sherri Schneider, *He's Just Not That Into You* (2004) by Greg Behrendt and Liz Tuccillo, and *Act Like A Lady, Think Like a Man* (2009) by Steve Harvey with Denene Miller.

The Rules

The Rules, which was followed by *The Rules II*, was quoted to have "revolutionized dating practices."* It first enjoyed pop culture status after it was the subject of a comedic skit on *Saturday Night Live* and later it influenced a sitcom adapted for television. After just skimming the book (I have three degrees, so I have perfected this art), it was clear to me that the premise for the entire publication was that hunting for a mate is a man's job. Grief!!

First, let me say that this idea was not news for women in the 90s. Even though the 60s' sexual revolution had empowered women to embrace their sexuality and, as a consequence, they became more confident and willing to pursue, it did not render them stupid. Women are intelligent, clever beings. In the 2001 movie, *Two Can Play that Game*, Anthony Anderson's character feeling challenged made this statement, "The CIA ain't got s- - - t on a woman with a plan!"*

Fein and Schneider must also have forgotten that we still look to "old school" experienced women like our grandmothers, mothers, aunts, and friends to hip us to the game.

Really, girls, who had not heard that you should never pursue a man? Or that you should never call a man. Or that it is best if a man desires you more. Or "why should a man buy the cow, if he can get the milk for free?" Or never be too serious or eager, but remain mysterious and keep him guessing.

Puh-leez! Revolutionary, my butt! Sorry. My momma gave me most of this advice and still...that's right, I am still single. Of course, there are reasons that we don't follow these words of supposed wisdom and that discussion could fill another chapter (hormones, impatience, thinking we know better).

That's the book in a nutshell, alongside endless lists of dos and don'ts when dating and other scenarios. Bottom line—do nothing and the man will choose you, pursue you, and marry you. It's his choice. Sounds a bit cave-mannish. Guess Fern and Schneider are not familiar with the lemonism (found in Chapter Five), "A man chases a woman until she catches him." Translated—a woman has a lot more to do with choosing her mate than even the man realizes.

By the way, one of my closest childhood girlfriends first saw her future husband in a photo at a neighbor's house and swore that she would marry him. I attended her 25th wedding anniversary celebration where they renewed their vows, and they now have been married for over 35 years. I guess she neglected to read her copy of *The Rules*.

He's Just Not That into You

Next on the chopping block is *He's Just Not That into You*, which reached its peak exposure in a movie of the same name, which grossed $90 million domestically.*

Hate to call it, but grief! The entire book is supported by survey answers from 10-20 persons and most of them are Behrendt's male friends. Can we talk conflict of interest? He makes an assertion and then presents his evidence based on unsubstantiated results. The number of men surveyed is a far cry from being a proper sampling of available eligible men in this country.

Both he and his co-writer Liz Tuccillo wrote for the popular HBO series *Sex in the City*. Seems to be like someone knew someone that knew someone and they get a book published and then a million-dollar movie. I ain't hating, but that doesn't make them experts on relationships.

Actually, the 40-something-year-old Liz Tuccillo has never gotten married herself as of the printing of this book. Looks like she may need to buy my book and learn to "make lemonade" since all the advice

Behrendt gave single women did her no good—at least not in snagging Mr. Right.

I must add though that getting women to the altar was not the intent of their collaboration. To sum it up, Behrendt just wanted to provide women with a reason (actually an excuse) for why men treat them horribly, lead them on, and then toss them to the side. They are just not that into them!

So, if they are not into us, why won't they be man enough to tell us the truth and move on until they find Mrs. Right? Don't hold your breath—that would make them human beings! Ouch! (Some of them just want the cake, the cookie, and the ice cream.) With all Behrendt's advice, you would still need to be telepathic to discern the mixed signals men often send.

Act Like a Lady, Think Like a Man

Steve Harvey's career gets resuscitated with the media onslaught of the best-selling book *Act Like a Lady, Think Like a Man* that he wrote with Denene Millner and the subsequent multi-million-dollar movies *Think Like a Man* and its sequel.*

The book was derived from the many hours Harvey spent responding to relationship questions from fans of his radio show. Harvey is willing, to the chagrin of many men all over the country, to reveal to women several truths about the men in their lives. Even though this is an upside to the book, I have to scream, "Grief!"

After Harvey fondly relays to us what a man needs, how to detect if a man loves you and how to get him to marry you, he lowers the boom.

Now at first, you're going through his instructions feeling empowered and feeling that you might just have a handle on this relationship thing and then you get to the section on WHY MEN CHEAT.* Talk about having the wind knocked out of your sails! Harvey insists that men cheat simply because they can.

Girls, we know from Chapter One that the odds are against total fidelity for either partner, even in marriage, but this revelation is earth-shaking. You see, Harvey implies that you can be a loving, supportive wife and still your husband will cheat simply because there is another human body willing, because they can get away with it, and because it is merely a physical act like going to the bathroom and dropping a load (those last words were mine and not Harvey's). Talk about a great selling point for my book!! Both the single woman and the 17% of married women about to be single (after getting a divorce) are gonna need it to survive!

That was so much fun! I know you're saying that I was a bit hard on all the authors. I did tell you upfront that they would be revenge reviews. But just as quickly as I wrote them from a "grief" perspective I could have gleaned areas in which each book offered some relief for the single woman. This detail is what I want you to keep in mind as you seek counsel from the thousands of resources offering you aid along this single life's journey. Remember, girls, that each source just offers a perspective, neither, completely right or wrong. It is up to you to distinguish personally which advice is grief and which is relief!

EPILOGUE

Girls, as I just shared in the previous chapter, there are so many voices and perspectives in this discussion about living single. For as many books and websites that I read, I still continued to discover others. Really, so much of it is fluff. During my writing I wasn't confident that I sounded any different from the crowd. I began to doubt if my effort would be relevant. You see, I genuinely wanted to add a realistic voice to all the noise—the rhetoric—telling you to do this and to do that. I wanted to tell my story and hope that it would resonate with single adult women of all ages. In fact, I didn't want to tell you to do anything, but to see yourself apart from all the expectations of society and the lives of people around you.

Hopefully, I didn't bite off more than I could chew. As Sanaa Lathan's character (Kenya) said in the movie, *Something New*, "Girl, don't fall for the hype!"[*]

I wanted you to embrace your uniqueness and then run for your life! You see, there are some miserable married folk and divorce ain't no joke!! That's not to say that there are no happy marriages, or should I say successful marriages.

Happiness is relative. Out of nine, I have four girlfriends that are still married to their first husbands after 20 plus years (that's about average), four that divorced (two of those remarried), and one that is a widow.

Then there is me (and my girl AW)—single, years past what I dreamed. It was tough! Sure, I learned to "make lemonade," to re-imagine my circumstances from decade to decade, but I did not want to be the only grandchild out of fifteen to remain single! Nor did I want to be 50-something wishing I had found some way to preserve my eggs. Of course, at the point that they were still viable, I could hardly afford the methods available for doing so.

That's the bitter truth. And so, we've come full circle back to the reasons I decided to have this intimate conversation with you—my sisters, some of you like my daughters. (I have single nieces and cousins that are 20 to 30-something-year-olds.) Hopefully you had a little fun, as I did, bashing the sacred life of "Mrs. Smith." Of course, the reality of domestic abuse is in no way comical.

Some sources state that the rush to the altar has tittered off, but the stats of the booming wedding business imply otherwise. Wall Street, through its mass communications' machinery, continues to drum into a woman's psyche that she's gotta have a man, a diamond, a marriage, a honeymoon, a home, and children. The significance of acquiring these status symbols is changing, but not enough to relieve women of the serious pressure obtaining them has always presented. The survey of college women which found that more than 80% of participants hoped to marry by thirty proves this.

Unfortunately, many will find it easy to identify with some of the challenges, frustrations, and stresses presented in Part I.

But those realities, which I chose to call the "lemons" of our single existence, are just half the story. I hope you, my mother, and Dale Carnegie think that I did a good job, "flipping the script" in Part II.

Everyone, including the "Mrs. Smiths" in our lives, experience frustration, disappointment, and loneliness. The key is to "make lemonade." In fact, girls, can we just make that the single woman's mantra? When times get tough, you face difficult trials alone, and you feel beat up by life, re-imagine the circumstances, "Make Lemonade!"

But I did more than just give lip service to this re-imagining thing. I provided you with a few practical life tools and strategies to implement along the journey. So if I meet you one day on the street, and say, "OMG, you're still single, so where the hell is your lemonade?" you should "represent" for us swl-lers by using some version of this reply:

"Well, I haven't met Mr. Right yet, or should I say that Mr. Right hasn't met me, but I am grateful to be alive and I have vowed to work, play, and serve others with passion, doing what I love to do whenever possible. I am working on strategies to realize my dreams and I don't long to be anyone else, I never imitate, because I like being me. I am not afraid to enjoy life on my own, if I have to—I deserve to!

The earth ain't never gonna shrink cuz of me, because I am gonna die fighting to fulfill my destiny!

Look at me, girl, ain't I FABULOUS? It's my own personalized grooming regimen that keeps me looking healthy, vibrant, and excited about being a woman. Yeah, my sex life could be better, (whose couldn't?) but I offset that with routine exercise, dancing the night away, and I make sure there's a lot of laughter in my life. Now, that's my lemonade, stirred and not shaken!"

Yeah, I know I got that last phrase backward. Intentionally. You know you don't shake lemonade. But don't you think that last line was a perfect ending for our empowered reply? You know I had to close making a final movie reference. What better way to end this conversation? It sounded like the swagger of James Bond. A bit ballsy, you say, but that response will come on a good day.

I never pretended that this book was a fix-all. You know, the thing I really wanted to do, I can't. I can't spare you the pain and disappointment that sometimes come with being single; no more than those close to me could. Then again, when I was younger, I never would have believed I would write a journal entry applauding my journey like this one that I rediscovered:

"It was almost spring…after my evening power walk and the noises from the apartment complex reminded me of days in the project where I grew up. Children were out playing, birds were singing, and dogs were barking. The cool breezes swept over me as I slowed my pace toward home.

I thought how wonderful it was to be alive. Even single. As I walked toward my building I stopped to watch the tennis players on the courts. I loved the spring and summer. This was it for me. I realized that I had gotten to do much of what I loved to do. I loved and played a lot of tennis. I had spent endless hours watching the game for years. I became the person I wanted to become and I am still evolving. I had a successful fashion career... I still could read into the wee hours of the night...I still had an insatiable desire to learn...I had danced nights away...I had had interesting romantic encounters...I had close family and friends all over the country...I had bought a convertible and the memory of nights riding around with the top down still made me smile...I still had a great passion for life and ambition enough to produce all the new versions of me that life will allow. I had had a heck of a ride!"

I guess y'all wanna ask, "All this from an evening walk?" (Those endorphins.) Yeah, I guess I live over the top. That's what making lemonade will do for you. You see after all is said and done, the ultimate goal is to come out on the other end whole...not bitter...potent...not some old maid...vibrant...fully alive!

So I want you to promise me something; promise me that you won't sit around waiting for something spectacular to happen, or wait for some big moment to occur like meeting Mr. Right before you decide to really live.

The big moment has already occurred, you took your first breath...you have permission to live life fully. Believe me, love, marriage, and children can occur anywhere along your journey. In fact, my sister-in-law, a surgical nurse said that the average age of women having babies is much higher than we would ever imagine—many mothers are in their fifties.

Plus—I wasn't gonna tell it—but I fell in love during the completion of this book and I mean it's the kind of heart-stopping, gut-wrenching sort. And I wasn't even expecting it! Sorry, can't say more, I'm saving it for my next book.

Ma-a-a-n, I really hate to go, girls. 'Know what they say, "All good things must come to an end." But hasn't this been a blast? You girls that are 20-something better know that you have the best opportunity for developing quality life since you're reading my book now. My 30-something sisters and daughters, it's tough but start immediately implementing my strategies and see what a difference it will make. You 40-something and over foxy, sophisticated chicks, LOL, should know that it ain't never over, just look at me, ain't I fabulous?!

I just hope you all think that I have contributed something valuable to the conversation about living single. You know that's the important thing; to keep having the conversation, to scream, to shout, to cry, get angry—but then to resolve to "make lemonade"; to re-imagine this single life until your status changes—or if not. And then to vow to live the hell out of it! Hope I have provided some tools to help you do that. I'm out, swl-lers! Luv ya.

ACKNOWLEDGMENTS

To God, who knows me best, (every flaw, every blemish) but still loves me; And to all the women in my family who came before me, you have inspired me to use every ounce of gift and talent I possess.

To my homeroom middle school teacher, whose revelation that I had a special way of writing both surprised and pleased me. To three of my college professors, William (Bill) Dinome, (Mount Olive College), Dr. Christopher Hudson, and Dr. Trevor Eppenheimer (Hood Theological Seminary), who all seemed to agree that I had "a way with words"—proof of which can be found in emails that I kept. Yeah, I needed to read them over and over again—to push myself to complete this manuscript.

To my fellow "hoodlums" (Class of 2010) at Hood Theological Seminary in Salisbury, North Carolina, who were the first to know that this book was a part of my life calling and to all those thereafter who didn't let me forget it.

To Doris Frazier, an aspiring poet and loving member of Greenville Memorial AMEZ Church in Charlotte, North Carolina, who was adamant that I should pursue writing after reviewing a sample of my work! She had no idea that this book was in the making. Her admonition to me was what I needed to return to writing after starting a dressmaking business. To Deborah Harper and Catherine Kearney—my sister friends—like me—born of the fish! They were the first persons near and dear to me that I wasn't afraid to tell about my desire to become an author.

To Maureen Ryan Griffin, award-winning writer, instructor, publisher, and creator of the website *WordPlay*, who spends most of her life encouraging others to write. Thank you; if it were not for you and the Charlotte-Mecklenburg Library (Morrison Regional), this book would have never been published.

To my dear associate-friend Jennifer Olsson, native of Wilmington, North Carolina, whose artistic talents have blessed me immeasurably since our days working for the NYT *Wilmington Star News*. Your support has been priceless!

And finally, to all the young and young-in-spirit single women who poured their hearts out to me as if they knew I needed assurance that there was a purpose for what my gut and soul kept urging me to produce.

THE "LEMON GLOSS"

BFF – best friend forever

CLAB – crying like a baby

G2G – got to go

JJ – just joking

LMHO – laughing my head off

LOL – laughing out loud

QL – quit laughing

ROI – return on investment

SETE – smiling ear to ear

SMH – shaking my head

SWL single while living

411 n. Most updated information.

kickback n. An informal gathering of people to relax and shoot the breeze.

lemonism n. An astute observation made by a man or woman derived from personal romantic experiences or from the experiences of others.

lemons n. The undesirable circumstances and issues that women confront living single.

make lemonade v. A catch phrase for single women to apply to the process of overcoming the undesirable circumstances and issues of their lifestyle, **syn.** re-imagine.

man chores n. Household and other tasks and duties that are traditionally designated for men.

personal rituals n. Social activities and experiences created to enhance a single woman's life when the more traditional social options are unavailable, **syn.** Plan B.

Plan A/B n. Plan A: social activities that women typically prefer to experience with significant others, friends, or family members in toe. Plan B: stand-ins, also known as personal rituals, for when Plan A is unavailable or fails.

radi-grats n. Unexpected occurrences of relief or pleasure during an ordinary day that can elevate an appreciation for life once they are recognized.

re-imagine v. The ability to rise above negative circumstances and use the energy to create a new positive reality; the ability to successfully cope with undesirable circumstances while pursuing one's life goals and aspirations; to evolve from one level of thinking to a greater understanding—from one state of being to another, **re-imagined, syn.** "make lemonade," "flip the script."

rejection fatigue n. A condition single women may experience after years of searching for Mr. Right and having little or no success.

swl-ler n. A woman who has never been married; A woman who is living single, **swl-ling v.**

FILMOGRAPHY

An Affair to Remember
Ever After, A Cinderella Story
I'm Gonna Get You Sucka
Picture Perfect
Hope Floats
Baggage Claim
Something Borrowed
Bridget Jones' Diary
The Purge
Love and Basketball
Hitch
The Mirror Has Two Faces
Stella Got Her Groove Back
Frozen
Mahogany
Two Can Play That Game
He's Just Not That into You
Think Like a Man
Something New
Goldfinger

ABOUT THE AUTHOR

Sheryl L. Bradford is a native of Wilmington, North Carolina. In 1980, she graduated with honors from N.C. Agricultural and Technical University in Greensboro, North Carolina receiving a B.S. Degree in Fashion Merchandising. She received a Master of Divinity Degree in 2010 from Hood Theological Seminary in Salisbury, North Carolina.

She enjoyed a successful 17-year career with Belk Stores Inc. at the location in Wilmington as a fashion buyer/department manager. Later she worked for the then NYT *Wilmington Star News* as an Advertising Sales Executive.

After relocating to Charlotte, North Carolina, in 2005 she fulfilled one of her dreams and started a dressmaking business. But she never gave up on her desire to become a writer and to share her experiences being single.

Soon after receiving her Master of Divinity Degree, she became an ordained minister. Although she has been single most of her adult life, she still believes in love, marriage and the pursuit of dreams.

Sheryl can be contacted at bradforddsheryl@gmail.com or Facebook.com/The Lemonade Memoir.

NOTES

See the corresponding asterisks on indicated pages within each section.

Introduction

17 **You know** Brown, Helen Gurley. *Sex and the Single Girl.* Fort Lee, N.J., Barricade Books, 07024, 2003, and (1962).

18 **The average** "Median Age at First Marriage-1890-2010, U.S. Bureau of the Census," www.infoplease.com/ipa/United States> U.S. Statistics>Marital Status-1890-2010.

19 **In fact** "Getting Married, Weddings Stats in the U.S." 15 November 2016, www.soundvision.com/article/wedding—statistics-in-the-U.S.html.

just take "Everything You Need to Know About Divorce." Wilkinson and Finkbeiner Family Law

Attorneys, 30 Nov. 2015, www.wf-lawyers.com/disvorce-statistics-and-facts.html.

20 **A survey** Hussar, April Daniels. "Survey: Most College Women Want to be Married by 30." *Self.* 30 August 2012, www.self.com/story/survey-most-college-women-want.html.
The Bachelor Marikir, Sheila. "The Top Reality TV Shows of the Decade." ABC News. 1 December 2009, abcnews.go.com/Entertainment/Decade/top-10-reality-tv-shows-decade/storyid.

21 **More than** "Statistics for Aids/African American Women, CDC Centers for Disease Control and Prevention, Health Equity-Women's Health, Leading Causes of Death in Females." 11 December 2014, www.cdc.gov/women/Icod/2013/WomenBlack-2013-pdf.html.
It's been Cooper, Brittany, "Black Girls Zero Sum Struggle," *Salon Magazine*, 6 March 2014, www.salon.com/2014/03/06/black_girls_zero/.

22 **And still** "Maya Angelou." Random House. 12 August 1978, www. Mayaangelou.com/books/Caged Bird Legacy, LLC. html.

24 "**When fate** Carnegie, Dale. "How to Stop Worrying and Start Living." www.westegg.com/u/r maintained/carnegie/stop-worry.html, 1948.

Part I: The Bitter Truth

31 **But snoring** Reyes, Jomvie, PTPP, RN, MN. "Why do Men Snore More than Women." Exploring Snoring. 13 October 2013, www.exploringsnoring.com/men-snore-women.html.

32 **During one** *Living Single*. Prod. Yvette Lee Bowser. Fox. Hollywood, Ca. 1993-98.

33 **It reminds me** *I'm Gonna Get You Sucka*. Dir. Keenan Ivory Wayans. Perfs. Bernie Casey, Anna Marie Johnson. MGM/UA Communications Co.,1988.

34 **She probably** www.soundvision.com
along with www.wf-lawyers.com
Women are www.marriagemissions.com
 By the Penn, Lisa. "Love Cheating Statistics: Do Men Cheat More than Women?" Your Tango. 7 June 2012, www.magazine.foxnews.com/love/cheating.

35 **But check** Kirschner, Diana PH. D. "Is Marriage Toxic to Women? Part II" *Psychology Today*. 2 March 2010, www.psychologytoday.com/Blog/finding-true-love/201003.
75% of Northrup, Chrisanna, Schwartz, Pepper, and Witte, James PHD. *The Normal Bar: The Surprising Secrets of Happy Couples and What They Reveal About Creating a New Normal*. N.Y., N.Y., Harmony Books, 2013.

39 **Sorrowfully, U.S**. National Network to End Domestic Violence. 28 Feb. 2017, www.nned.org/getinvolved/dvam/1307-dvam-blog-series-1.

39 **Also, one** IBID.

48 **You know** www.soundvision.com

49 **Actress, Jennifer** *Picture Perfect.* Dir. Glenn Gordon
Caron. Perfs. Jennifer Anniston, Jay Mohr. 3 Arts
Entertainment, 1997.
In a *Baggage Claim.* Dir. David E. Talbert. Perfs. Paula
Patton, Derek Luke. 20th Century Fox, 2013.

50 **The women** Walsh, Jonathan P. "Melmouth, The
Wanderer," Japanese Cultural Glossary, 1 April 1998,
www.redbrick.dcu.le/~melmoth/japan/l.html.

53 **Dr. Tony** Evans Th.D., Anthony T. *Single and Satisfied,
How Singles Can Cope with Sexuality.* Dallas, TX, The
Urban Alternative, Inc., 1990.

55 **that most** Marantz, Robin. "What's the 'Best Age' to
Have a Baby?" *Psychology Today.* 20 Nov. 2012,
www.psychologytoday.com/blog/cusp/2012/html.

56 **In the** *Something Borrowed.* Dir. Luke Greenfield. Perfs.
Kate Hudson, Ginnifer Goodwin. Warner Home
Video, 2011.
Sorry about *Bridget Jones' Diary.* Dir. Sharon Maguire.
Perfs. Renee Zellweger, Colin Firth. Miramax/Universal
Films, 2001.

57 **(Check out** Patton, Susan. *Marry Smart, Advice for
Finding the One.* N.Y., N.Y., 10020, Gallery Books, 2014.
Since the www.wf-lawyers.com
Remember the *Just Wright,* Dir. Sanaa Hamri. Perfs.
Queen Latifah, Common. 20th Century Fox Century
Home Entertainment, 2010.

58 **According to** Dahl, Melissa, "Get Married in Your Late
20s If You Rather Not Get Divorced." Science of Us.

NY Magazine. 20 June 2015, nymag.com/science of us/2015/best-age-to-get-married.html.

Despite the Beyoncé. "Put a ring on it." I am...Sasha Fierce. Exec. Prods. Beyoncé Knowles/Matthew Knowles for Music World Prods. Inc., 2008.

59 **and most** 2010 U.S. Bureau of the Census, www.infoplease.com/ipa/United States>U.S. Statistics>Marital Status-1890-2010.

61 **Now, girls** *How Stella Got her Groove Back.* Dir. Kevin Rodney Sullivan. Perfs. Angela Bassett, Whoopi Goldberg. 20th Century Fox, 1998.

68 **Nor can** Smith, Alexander McCall. *The Limppo Academy of Private Detection, The No. 1 Ladies Detective Agency.* N.Y., N.Y., Pantheon Books, 2012. 245.

70 **Have you** Three 6 Mafia ft. Paula Campbell. "It's Hard Out Here for a Pimp." Hustle and Flow. Warner/Chappell Music Inc. BMG Rights Mgt. US LLC., 2005.

71 **Even nursery** Jack and Jill, English Nursery Rhyme. Roud #10266. www.wikipedia.org/wiki/Jack-and Jill-(nursery-rhyme).html.

72 **One scene** *Hitch,* Dir. Andy Tennant. Perfs. Will Smith, Eva Mendes. Columbia Pictures Industries, 2005.

73 **Yes we** 5th Dimension. "One Less Bell." Portrait. Writers, Hal David/Burt Bacharach. Warner/Chappell Music Inc., 1970.

76 **"I don't** Behrendt, Greg and Tuccillo. Liz, *He's Just Not That into You.* N.Y., N.Y., Simon and Schuster Inc., 2004, 56.

77 **AARP reports** Cullinaire, Jan. *AARP, The Single Woman's Guide to Retirement.* Waterville, Me., Thorndike Press, 2013.
Pastor Stenneth Powell, Stenneth. *What to Do Before You Say "I Do."* Denver, Colorado, Legacy Publishers International, 2003.

79 **Sharing ourselves** Brady, John. *Frank and Ava.* Thomas Dunne Books, St. Martin's Press, N.Y., 2015. 171.

81 **This scene** *Love and Basketball*, Dir. Gina Prince-Bythewood. Perfs. Omar Epps, Sanaa Lathan. New Line Home Video/New Line Production Inc., 2000.

82 **In my** Wilcox, Melanie. "Why Romance Novels Turn Women On." Acculturated Pop Culture Matters. 9 July 2016, www.acculturated.com/why-romance-novels-turn-women-on/html.
Because while *The Mirror Has Two Faces*, Dir. Barbra Streisand. Perfs. Barbra Streisand, Jeff Bridges. Columbia TriStar video, 1997.

83 **And Natalie** Natalie Cole, Diana Krall, "Better Than Anything." Ask A Woman Who Knows. Writers, Bill Louborough/David Wheat, The Verve Music Group, 2002.

84 **Susan Patton** Susan Patton

85 **After what** Gray, John PH.D. *Men are from Mars, Women are from Venus.* N.Y., N.Y., Harper Collins, 1992.

89 **In 2012** Penn, Charlie. "Black Love: Barack and Michelle Obama's Most Romantic Moments." *Essence*

Magazine. 01 October 2012, essence.com/black-love-barack-and-michelle/html.

91 **First, the** The Righteous Brothers. "You've Lost That Lovin Feelin." Loving Who You With. Prod. /Writer, Phil Spector, 2007.

94 **Not too** *Frozen,* Dirs. Jennifer Lee, Chris Buck. Perfs. Kristen Bell, Idina Menzel. Disney Video, 2013.

Part II: From Bitter to Sweet

101 **You know** Ehrlich, Amy. Adapted. *The Random House Book of Fairy Tales.* N.Y., N.Y., Random House, 1985.

102 **This film** Stewart, Andrew. "*Frozen* Reaches 1.219 Billion to Become Fifth Highest Grossing Film Globally." *Variety.* 25 May 2014, www.variety.com/2014film/box-office/frozen/reached -1-219-bil.html.

110 **Yeah, I** *Mahogany*, Dir. Berry Gordy. Perfs. Diana Ross, Billie Dee Williams. Paramount Pictures, 1975. **Once, during** Pollard, William L. Dr. "Servanthood," Presidential Inauguration. Hood Theological Seminary, 2 Oct. 2014. Salisbury, N.C. Address.

111 **Keep you** Campbell, Deena. "Eddie Glaude Jr.," *Uptown Magazine.* 27 July 2010, www.Uptown Magazine.com.html.

121 **One useful** *Hope Floats*, Dir. Forest Whitaker. Perfs. Sandra Bullock, Harry Connick Jr. Twentieth Century Fox, 1998.

132 **Speaking of** Millner, Denene, *The Sistahs' Rules*. N.Y., N.Y., 10019, William Morrow and Co. Inc. 1997. 98.
And just Helen Gurley Brown

133 **Now, one** Schnarch PH.D, David. *Resurrecting Sex.* N.Y., N.Y., HarperCollins Publishers, 2002, 62.
I guess, Jio, Sarah, "10 things You Didn't Know about Orgasms." *Woman's Day.* 2 June 2016, www.woman'sday.com/relationships/sex-tips/a5144/10-surprising-facts-about-orgams-111985html.
But get IBID.
Sexual therapist Westheimer, Ruth K. Dr., Lehu, Pierre A. *The doctor Is In: Dr. Ruth on Love, Life and Joie de Vivre.* N.Y., N.Y., Amazon Publishing, 2015, 54.
The French IBID. 55.

136 **You must** Angelou, Maya. Tom Joyner Morning Show WOSF-FM. 105.3. 28 March 2006. Charlotte, N. C. Interview.

138 **Dr. Ruth** Ruth Westheimer, 55.
I know Hughes, Langston. "Mother to Son." *The Collected Poems of Langston Hughes."* Vintage Books, 1994,,www.poetryfoundation.org/poem=poets/detail47559html.

141 **In the** Quan, Cipriana. www.essence.com, September 2014, 68.

143 **A lot** "Gen Elle on Life, Love and Work," *Elle Magazine*, September 2015, 240-244.

151 ***The Rules*** Fein, Ellen, and Schneider, Sherrie. *The Rules II, More Rules to Live and Love By.* N.Y., N.Y, 10020, Warner Books, Inc. 1997. 8, 11.

The CIA *Two Can Play That Game.* Dir. Mark Brown. Perfs. Vivica A. Fox, Morris Chestnut. Columbia Tristar Home Entertainment, 2001.

153 **Next on** Greg Behrendt, Liz Tuccillo

154 **Steve Harvey** Harvey, Steve, Millner, Denene. *Act Like a Lady, Think Like a Man.* N.Y., N.Y., Harper Collins, 2009.

155 **Now at** IBID, 95.

157 **As Sanaa** *Something New.* Dir. Sanaa Hamri. Perfs. Sanaa Lathan, Simon Baker. Universal Home Entertainment, 2006.

160 **Now, that's** *Goldfinger.* Dir. Guy Hamilton. Perfs. Sean Connery, Gert Frobe. United Artists, 1964.

www.ingramcontent.com/pod-product-compliance
Lightning Source LLC
Chambersburg PA
CBHW051826040426
42447CB00006B/387